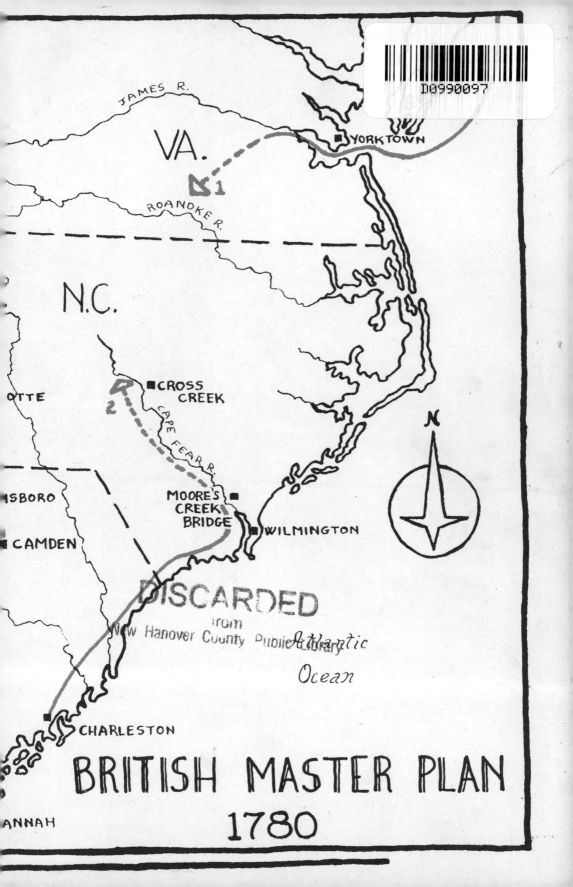

King's Mountain

King's Mountain

The Epic of the Blue Ridge "Mountain Men"
in the American Revolution

by

Hank Messick

Little, Brown and Company / Boston / Toronto

FIRST EDITION

T 04/76

The author is grateful to the University of Chicago Library for
permission to quote from *The Autobiography of Isaac Shelby,*
Reuben T. Durrett Collection, Codex 165.

Library of Congress Cataloging in Publication Data
Messick, Hank
  King's Mountain.
  Bibliography: p.
    1. Kings Mountain, Battle of, 1780.   I.   Title
E241.K5M47   973.3'36   75-42425
ISBN 0-316-56796-5

Design by D. Christine Benders

Published simultaneously in Canada
by Little, Brown & Company (Canada) Limited

PRINTED IN THE UNITED STATES OF AMERICA

For Mildred
in Happy Valley

On the site of the Battle of King's Mountain, amid oak trees and silence, stands
a marble obelisk erected by the United
States of America. Upon its side these
words appear:

THIS BRILLIANT VICTORY MARKED THE TURNING
POINT OF THE AMERICAN REVOLUTION

Preface

The Revolutionary War in the southern states has received little attention in comparison to the detailed study given the campaigns in the North. This is unfortunate since much decisive action took place there, but perhaps the nature of the struggle accounts for the historians' neglect. The heroes of the southern fighting were not the officers of the Continental army but rather the natural leaders of the people, who had learned their skills in the continuing effort to seize the land of the Indians.

By achieving better perspective of the past, something may be accomplished in the present. For the hero of this book has fallen on evil times. He is called various unflattering names today and is the butt of comic-strip buffoonery and the "villain" of serious novels. Because he remains an individualist, he is a safe target.

There's nothing new about this attitude, of course. In the Revolutionary War period, he was sneered at by the rich merchants of the lowlands, he was held in contempt by the Continental Army's high command, and he was considered less than human by the British. Major Patrick Ferguson called him a bandit, a barbarian, a mongrel. He had little respect for law and order. He could be quite ruthless. He was also superstitious and at times naive. Yet Theodore Roosevelt could write of him:

"The fathers followed Boone or fought at King's Mountain; the sons marched south with Jackson to overcome the Creeks; the grandsons died at the Alamo."

And, it should be added, the great-grandsons provided Lee and Johnson with the best fighting infantry the world had yet seen. Poorly clothed, half-starved, they responded magnificently to magnificent leadership and almost won America's second civil war as their forefathers had won the first.

Moreover, in wars since, they have always been the cutting edge. As F. N. Boney, the Georgia historian, puts it: "There is no shortage of rednecks in the neat, quiet American military cemeteries which now dot the globe. However rejected in normal times, the redneck has always been welcomed when the nation went to war."

Peace is the dream today, and the redneck shares that dream. For him it was often a "rich man's war and a poor man's fight." He never started a war, but he was always ready when his home and personal liberty were threatened. And because of the readiness to do his duty as he saw it, this nation was founded and kept alive.

Prejudices I surely possess, since I was born in Happy Valley on the upper Yadkin in the foothills of the Blue Ridge. As a boy I visited Fort Defiance and saw the Spanish sword William Lenoir brought home from King's Mountain. I also visited the family cemetery and tried to read the words cut in the moss-encrusted stone above Lenoir's grave. As a youth I helped survey power lines for rural-electric cooperatives in the coves and hollows of Watauga County, and I walked the war trails of the ancient Cherokees. The desire to tell the story of King's Mountain developed early.

Later, as a reporter for the *Courier-Journal* in Louisville, my ambition broadened when "sophisticated" reporters, born and raised in New York, explored the Kentucky hills and returned to the city room to laugh. They thought the hillbilly custom of putting his new refrigerator on the front porch stemmed from vanity, never realizing that the front porch was the only vacant space in the cabin. Until electricity came to the mountains, there had been little change for generations in the domestic arrangements of the mountaineer, but abruptly he had to find room for new appliances and even an indoor bathroom. The front porch was an ideal solution.

What those young reporters, interning for a couple of years in Kentucky before returning to the big time, had trouble comprehending was the basic fact that the hillbilly, by and large, is not interested in the fast buck. Wealth has never appealed to him as an end in itself. If he expects a reward for hard work, he assumes it will come in heaven. He still practices the Protestant Ethic, you see. More important to him than money is his personal freedom, the right to do something or nothing as he pleases. His poverty, even his ignorance, stems not from laziness or stupidity but indifference.

I remember a conversation some years ago in Newport, Kentucky, a city founded on the old salt licks where the Licking River enters the Ohio. Some citizens there were in revolt against a crime syndicate that had made the town into the largest gambling center east of Las Vegas. I was there as a reporter. With me that night was Ed Hill, "the tamer of bloody Harlan," a county in the Kentucky mountains famous for feuds and coal-mine violence. As circuit judge, Hill had brought back respect for law to Harlan, and, in doing so, had won some respect for himself. He was in Newport to conduct a special grand jury probe of crime and corruption. I asked him, one hillbilly to another and off the record, why he wasn't afraid of the syndicate punks who had strutted about the dark and dirty Ohio River city for two decades. The judge poured the bourbon.

"Hank," he said, "before coming up here I had a chat with some of the fellows in Harlan. They said they'd get the word out that if anybody gave me any trouble they'd come up and clean out the town."

He smiled without humor. "One thing about the fellows back home — when they say they're going to kill somebody, they kill him."

The example set by Judge Hill inspired both the grand jurors and the citizens of Newport. The latter came forth to testify and the jurors voted indictments by the score. The day came when Judge Hill said to me: "Our job's done."

Given proper leadership, the mountain man can still be motivated. But in recent years such leadership has been largely lacking. The potential remains untapped, but it is there. As my father used to say in Happy Valley—you may turn the damper up, you may turn the damper down, but the smoke goes up the chimney just the same.

Hank Messick

Peace River,
Arcadia

Prologue
Monongahela

It was a pretty sight until the first war whoop sounded.

The British army was stretched out for 1,900 yards along a twelve-foot corridor hacked out by an advance guard. To the left was some underbrush along the edge of the river and to the right was a wooded hill. Straight ahead was Fort Duquesne, less than eight miles away. Tomorrow, July 9, 1755, the fort would crumble under the siege guns hauled over the mountains and the decisive battle of the French and Indian War would be won. Such, at least, was the hope.

The afternoon sun was bright, the drums beat cheerfully, and the woodland — more like a park than a forest — gleamed with color: the scarlet of uniforms, the white tops of the covered wagons, the burnished steel of bayonets. Everywhere flags flew as the men moved confidently forward. General Edward Braddock had caused the army to detour over the Monongahela and then recross it upstream. If the hapless French and their Indian allies had planned to make a fight outside the fort, surely they would have contested one or both of the crossings. Now the route ahead was a parade ground to victory.

George Washington, one of Braddock's aides, felt much better. He had been gravely ill for several days and had feared he might miss the victory at the end of the long trail. The crossing of the river had been glorious to behold — one of the "most thrilling" sights in his young life. It appeared that, despite all the doubts of the "colonials" attached to the army, Braddock's military experience had proved itself. The army had crawled along through the wilderness in textbook order, just as it would have done on the plains of Europe, protecting its supplies, its artillery, and even its women. Of the latter, the quota per company had been cut from six to two because of the rigors of the march. The enemy had been there all along, but aside from picking off and scalping an occasional straggler, there had been little it could do. Now Braddock was bearing down on vital Fort Duquesne with an overwhelming weight of men and metal. With him were only a handful of Indians, but he considered them worthless — almost as worthless as the militia. Who needed them?

Among the men so lightly regarded was a youth named Daniel Boone. He had enjoyed the campaign, spending his free time listening to a hunter named John Finley tell tall tales of a happy hunting ground beyond the Blue Ridge called "Caintuck." Back with the wagons was a giant of a man, a lusty brawler with a tender back named Daniel Morgan. For insulting a British officer he had been given a formal lashing, but, he boasted, the drummer missed a beat and the King owed him another lash.

Up front was Colonel Thomas "Honest Tom" Gage, a future commander in chief of the British army. Now he was in command of the advance unit. Reaching a wide clearing and noting the sun was dipping low, Gage ordered his men to halt. The army would camp there and push on next day to the fort at the forks of the Ohio.

The word to stop had scarcely passed Gage's lips when war whoops rang out, and a volley of shots echoed through the woods. Gage, who was wounded in the battle, later admitted he saw only one enemy during the entire affair. The screams of the

Indians as well as the bullets they fired seemed to come out of nowhere.

Braddock, with Washington at his side, was back with the rear guard near the river when the shooting began. He put spurs to his horse and galloped forward to see what was happening. His men were firing all along the line, firing blindly at an invisible enemy which was now peppering the stalled army from both flanks as well as from the front.

The reason the attack was so late wasn't one of design. The French had been unable to persuade their Indian allies to assault Braddock's impressive force with inferior numbers. At last in desperation some 250 white men — regulars and militia — marched out of Fort Duquesne dressed for bush fighting — in breechclouts and leggings. The Indians were shamed into joining, and the little army of nine hundred men moved under the command of Captain Daniel-Hyacinthe-Marie Lienard de Beaujeu. By then it was too late to catch the British at the river fords. Beaujeu signaled to the Indians to envelop the enemy on the right and left while the French held the center.

The battle was almost lost a few seconds after it began. One of the British volleys into thin air hit Beaujeu and killed him. The Indians, who were there only because they admired the fallen captain, turned to run. Captain Jean-Daniel Dumas took command, however, and turned a near rout into an angry charge. Anxious now to avenge Beaujeu, the Indians began whooping again. Their screams were as effective as their bullets in terrifying British soldiers completely unaccustomed to such sounds.

Gage, unable to advance against the French center, ordered his men to fall back on the main army. A mistake. The retreating men ran headlong into the vanguard of the larger force which had been sent forward on the double to help Gage. Great confusion resulted. It grew as the Indians on the right slipped along the hill and fired point-blank into the huddled mass of men on the little road.

The Americans in the army defied conventional military wis-

xv

dom and broke ranks to fight from tree to tree. One detachment tried to take the hill itself. Unhappily, the British mistook them for the enemy in the smoke and panic. Happy to have a target, they blasted away at their allies and killed many of them. The incident did nothing to improve later working relations between the two groups.

Braddock, brave, stubborn and stupid, rushed madly about, screaming curses at his men, hitting them with his sword, trying to bring order out of increasing chaos. Four horses were shot from under him, but he always remounted. Now a bullet hit his right arm and penetrated his body. He reeled in the saddle and was lifted to the ground. Conscious still, he gave orders impossible to execute. No one listened.

Suddenly, the sound of heavy firing near the rear of the column startled the leaderless troops. Word spread that they were about to be surrounded. Abruptly, the rout was on. According to Washington, the men "broke and ran as sheep pursued by dogs." Efforts to stop them met "with as little success as if we had attempted to have stopped the wild boars of the mountains." The wagons, the guns, the women were abandoned as the troops rushed to the river. Luckily for them, the Indians paused to plunder and scalp; there was no pursuit.

Out of a force of 1,459 officers and men, 456 were dead and 421 were wounded. Washington's clothes had been riddled and two horses had been killed beneath him, but he was without a scratch. Among the wounded was Captain Horatio Gates.

Braddock was still alive. He ordered a retreat and rode in a wagon for four jolting days, lucid much of the time but no longer attempting to command. Daniel Morgan was there when Braddock told his men:

"We shall better know how to deal with them another time."

Braddock died on the evening of July 13, 1755, and Washington ordered a trench dug in the road at the head of the column; there the fallen general was buried. The survivors marched over him, tramping down the earth so that no Indian could find the body and perhaps scalp it.

Braddock's successor, although still comanding a formidable force, retreated to Philadelphia and left the frontier undefended. The French and Indians carried fire and tomahawk over much of Virginia and Pennsylvania until the settlers began banding together in "private" forts to defend themselves.

The lesson Braddock learned, the lesson he hoped would be useful "another time," was ignored by the British army. Even Washington, who was trying to build a military career of a conventional kind, remained a textbook soldier. But frontiersmen like Morgan profited. Another generation of fighting would be necessary before the American developed the skills, the ruthlessness, that would make him a match for the Indian. When at last he was able to cross the blue mountains and survive, he felt confident enough to assert his independence of the British empire he had helped build.

The lesson the British did not learn at Monongahela was taught again at King's Mountain.

A Partial Chronology of Events with Which This Book Is Concerned

1755

JULY 9 —

French and Indians teach British and Americans a bloody lesson in Battle of Monongahela.

1771

MAY 16 —

Battle of Alamance separates the men from the boys as Regulator movement is crushed in North Carolina.

1774

OCTOBER 10 —

At Battle of Point Pleasant, the Backwater Men prove to Shawnees that they've come of age as fighters.

1775

MARCH 17 —

Cherokees sell Kentucky and the lands along the Watauga at big gathering on the river.

1776

FEBRUARY 27 —

Highland Scots rise in support of British and are defeated at Moore's Creek Bridge by Patriot militia.

JULY 20 —

Watauga men defeat Cherokees at Island Flats as war rages all along the frontier. In September, combined forces of three states invade and ravage the Cherokee Nation.

1780

MARCH 29 —

British attack Charleston as war returns to the South.

MAY 11 —

Charleston and the only Continental army in the South surrender to British.

MAY 29 —

Col. Banastre Tarleton slaughters Patriot detachment at Waxhaws, and makes "Tarleton's quarter" a synonym for butchery.

JUNE 5 —

Sir Henry Clinton sails north, leaving the British army in the South in the hands of Lord Charles Cornwallis.

JUNE 20 —

Patriots defeat Tories at Ramseur's Mill.

JULY 14 —

Pacolet fight where Noah Hampton is murdered.

JULY 30 —

Isaac Shelby wins battle of Fort Thickety.

AUGUST 16 —

Cornwallis destroys American army under Gen. Gates at Camden, leaving South seemingly in his hands.

AUGUST 18 —

Shelby and his hillbillies win decisively at Musgrove Mill, but flee toward the mountains on hearing of Camden.

SEPTEMBER 7 —

Maj. Patrick Ferguson invades North Carolina as part of Cornwallis's master plan to end the war.

SEPTEMBER 15 —

Ferguson reaches headwaters of the Catawba River at the foot of the Blue Ridge.

SEPTEMBER 18 —

Col. Charles McDowell's retreat before Ferguson ends at Sycamore Shoals on the Watauga River near present-day Elizabethton, Tennessee.

SEPTEMBER 20 —

Cornwallis's main army reaches Charlotte, where he pauses while supplies come up.

SEPTEMBER 25 —

The Backwater Men rendezvous at Sycamore Shoals and vow to "git" Ferguson.

SEPTEMBER 26 —

Inspired by the prayers of the Rev. Samuel Doak, the volunteer army begins its march across the mountains.

SEPTEMBER 27 —

Backwoodsmen climb above the clouds and cross Roan Mountain in the snow as two desert to warn Ferguson.

OCTOBER 1 —

East side of the mountains reached and junction made with Wilkes and Surrey County men under Col. Ben Cleveland. Ferguson issues his "Pissing Proclamation."

OCTOBER 4 —

Col. William Campbell of Virginia takes nominal command of Patriot army, and Ferguson retreats toward Charlotte.

OCTOBER 5 —

Patriots reach Green River, make contact with various reinforcements.

OCTOBER 6 —

Mountain men "streamline" their army, leaving footmen behind, and begin desperate drive to catch Ferguson. Stop at Hannah's Cowpens for a quick dinner and push on through rainy night upon learning that Ferguson has camped on King's Mountain.

OCTOBER 7 —

March ends in mid-afternoon. Battle of King's Mountain. Ferguson is slain and all his men killed or captured.

OCTOBER 8 —

Retreat toward the mountains begins.

OCTOBER 14 —

Cornwallis begins retreat from Charlotte in great confusion, ending the first invasion of North Carolina.

NOVEMBER 16 —

Col. John Sevier defeats the Cherokees at Boyd's Creek after recrossing the mountains with his men.

1781

JANUARY 17 —

Gen. Daniel Morgan with help from the King's Mountain men, defeats Tarleton at Cowpens.

OCTOBER 19 —

Cornwallis surrenders at Yorktown.

Contents

King's Mountain

1

To a Far and Distant Land

Of first importance were the mountains, shimmering like a blue haze on the northwestern horizon, at once challenging and reassuring with their hint of mystery and their promise of eternity.

In the beginning, say the legends of the Cherokees, the waters covered the earth. When they receded, large islands were exposed. The Great Buzzard took flight on a journey of exploration. Upon reaching the land of the Cherokee, he tired and dropped so low his wings beat upon the earth. On every downstroke a valley appeared, on every upstroke a mountain. The animals became worried, fearing the whole world would become mountainous, and they persuaded the Great Buzzard to alight and rest.

The Cherokees say the first white men to reach the mountains were from Wales. They landed, according to the great chief Oconostota, at the point where Mobile stands today, and moved inland. The Cherokees drove them west. Similar stories were cited by early English writers to justify their country's claim to the area. Others have insisted that the first settlers were members of the Lost Tribes of Israel. One enterprising baronet tried to establish a homeland for Jews in the mountains of the south.

Legends aside, when de Soto arrived in 1540, the Cherokees were there — from northern Alabama and Georgia through the western parts of North and South Carolina and into Virginia. Their homes were the mountain fastnesses and there they seemed invincible. No enemy existed to the east. To the west was a broad strip of neutral ground which men of all tribes could hunt but none control.

The white man brought disease. In 1738 the population of the Cherokee Nation — then estimated at 15,000 — was cut in half by smallpox. Many outlying areas were abandoned to the buffalo, the wolf, and the white trapper.

Wild and wonderful were the mountains. The northern range came to be known as the Blue Ridge, the southern as the Great Smokies. Mount Mitchell towered 6,684 feet high, tallest peak east of the Mississippi, and there were other giants: Clingman's Dome, 6,643; Roan High Knob, 6,313; and Grandfather, 5,984. The lower elevations were covered with hardwoods: chestnut, oak, maple, hickory, and locust. Near the top would be spruce and balsam and perhaps a "rhododendron hell"— a jungle of underbrush so thick man could not penetrate. The tops of many mountains were bald; trees had ceased to grow and grass covered the ground.

It was into such territory as this that Bishop August Spangenberg, of the Protestant sect then known as the Renewed Unitas Fratrum and today as the Moravians, came in search of land for his gentle people. On November 19, 1752, he camped at Quaker Meadows on the Catawba and ten days later he reached "a region that has perhaps been seldom visited since the creation of the world." Six days after that he climbed an "indescribably steep mountain" to the crest of the Blue Ridge. In his diary he noted:

"When we reached the top we saw mountains to right and to left, before and behind us, many hundreds of mountains, rising like great waves in a storm."

4

The bishop and his party wandered for several days in search of the Yadkin River, which flows eastward out of the Blue Ridge and then turns southward through the Carolinas to the Atlantic Ocean. They didn't find it. Likewise, they missed the headwaters of the Watauga, which rises a dozen miles from the birthplace of the Yadkin to flow northwestward into the Holston and then west to the Tennessee and the Ohio. They also missed the North Toe River, which almost spills over the eastern side of the Blue Ridge before cutting north to become the Nolichucky and join the French Broad. But they did find another river and they followed it in the forlorn hope "that it would lead us out." This proved to be the New River, which flows north through the Virginias to merge with the Ohio.

Bishop Spangenberg finally decided to leave the river and steer a course "between east and south." It brought him across the mountain sea to the Yadkin near the present site of Wilkesboro. Some eighty miles down the winding river he founded his settlement near the present site of Winston-Salem. "If we had had a true account of this in the beginning," the bishop wrote, "perhaps we would not have gone to the Catawba nor beyond the Blue Mountains to the New River."

The region visited by Bishop Spangenberg was in the next two decades to become the home and hunting grounds of men who became known to legend as the Long Hunters, the Men of the Western Waters, and Backwater Men. Call them mountaineers or frontiersmen too, if you like, or Shirtmen or Yelling Devils, as the British did. Perhaps riflemen says it best. The name isn't as important as the men.

Avenues into the hills were the Valley of Virginia from the northeast and the Yadkin Valley from the southeast. Eventually, in defiance of royal governors and hostile Indians, the pioneers pushed through the mountain passes and founded new states. Many of them were Scotch-Irish. The term is geographical and refers to Lowland Scots who were transplanted by James I of England to the province of Ulster in Ireland. Beginning in 1607, more than 30,000 Scots were resettled and became the majority in Ulster. They prospered and by 1700 were competing with English industry. Repressive measures to reduce their competition were taken and when after a hundred years their long-term leases expired, landlords demanded higher rents. A smallpox epidemic and a potato crop failure added to the woes and sent thousands to America. By 1740, more than 12,000 people were leaving Ireland each year. By 1768, an estimated 200,000 had fled the Emerald Isle.

While some immigrants worked their way up from Charleston, most of the Scotch-Irish debarked in Philadelphia and moved down the Great Wagon Road to the area around Winston-Salem. With their skills as farmers, hunters, and artisans, they brought an ability to make good whiskey. In the "bottom land" of mountain streams they grew corn in excess of normal needs, and combined it with pure water to produce "white lightning." It was high quality and valuable since, unlike excess corn, it could be stored indefinitely. In a world where specie was scarce, corn whiskey became a currency. It could be traded for anything except, perhaps, taxes, but a few drinks would put even the tax collector into a mellow mood. And the backwoodsman felt he had a *right* to make whiskey just as he had a *right* to plant corn. In years to come he was to resist attempts to restrict that right.

"Truculent and obstinate," Theodore Roosevelt called him, but Roosevelt added: "Full credit has been awarded the Round-head and the Cavalier for their leadership in our history; nor have we been altogether blind to the deeds of the Hollander and the Huguenot; but it is doubtful if we have wholly realized the importance of the part played by that stern and virile people, the Irish whose preachers taught the creed of Knox and Calvin . . . Mingled with the descendants of many other races, they nevertheless formed the kernel of the distinctively and intensely American stock who were the pioneers of our people in their march westward."

While not so numerous as the Scotch-Irish, the so-called "Pennsylvania Dutch" joined the assault on the mountains. Their ancestors had come from Germany a generation before, settling around Philadelphia. About 1747 they started down the Great Wagon Road — America's north–south boulevard — and settled along the Yadkin and the Catawba. In the year 1765 alone, a thousand wagons passed through Salisbury and headed west.

Adding seasoning to this ethnic stew were some French Huguenots whose fathers reached Virginia around 1705. Things were crowded there and soon the sons pushed west in search of living space.

Elbow room was the goal of all new arrivals. It was no longer available in the tidal areas. Of eastern North Carolina, Bishop Spangenberg wrote: "The land that we have seen is not particularly good, and yet we are told that it has all been taken up; I presume this is so, for, otherwise, people would not go two hundred miles further west to settle."

There was great hunger in these refugees from Europe — great hunger for land of their own. Each acquisition made larger dreams possible. The pioneers who settled the rich valleys of the Yadkin soon were thinking of all that uncrowded land beyond the blue mountains. And such men as Christopher Gist and Daniel Boone went looking.

Around 1750, Gist wandered to the falls of the Ohio where Louisville stands. He brought home to the Yadkin a mammoth's tooth said to weigh four pounds. In his absence the Cherokees had raided his property, causing his family to flee to Roanoke. But Gist went back — and became a scout for the youthful George Washington in the days when the enemy was French. Gist is credited with saving Washington's life on several occasions.

When the French were beaten, British policy changed. A royal proclamation was issued in 1763 forbidding expansion beyond the Blue Ridge. A north-south line running from Canada to the Floridas along the mountain crest was drawn. All claims to lands west of the line were annulled and no private person could obtain title. Permission from the King was required even to visit beyond the blue hills, since the western lands were reserved exclusively for the Indian.

7

In a letter dated November 10, 1770, Thomas Gage, British commander in North America, tried to justify the policy by declaring: "There is room enough for the colonists to spread within our present limits for a century to come." In other words, the British hoped to make the eastern seaboard resemble Britain's "tight little isle" with all that implied in the way of economic and political control. Gage feared that expansion would bring economic independence. "When," he added, "all connections upheld by commerce with the mother country shall cease, it may be suspected that an independency on her government shall follow." The people, he added, "want no encouragement to desert the seacoasts and go into the back countries where the lands are better and got upon easier terms. They are already almost out of reach of law and government," he concluded. "Neither the endeavors of government or fear of Indians has kept them properly within bounds."

Gage went on to express the fear that if the Indians were driven from their forests, the wilderness "might become the asylum of fugitive Negroes and idle vagabonds." This view perhaps explains the attitude of those British officers some years later who considered patriots from the mountains to be mongrels and barbarians.

By their unwillingness to permit "law and government" to spread into the back country, the British almost invited rebellion. The Reverend Charles Woodmason, an Anglican cleric, described lawless conditions in a petition to authorities. Not only was thievery and vandalism rife, he said, but "married women have been ravished, virgins deflowered, and other unheard of cruelties committed by these barbarous ruffians." Moreover, he continued, there was no security for the merchant, no legal processes for the collection of debts, and no churches in which to publish banns or ministers to perform marriage ceremonies. "Thus we live and have lived for years past as if without God in the world, destitute of the means of knowledge or gospel, esteem or credit. For we know not even the laws of this country we

8

inhabit, for where are they to be found but in the secretary's office in Charleston."

But if things were bad in South Carolina, where the cleric lived, they were even worse to the north. Reverend Woodmason wrote: "The manners of the North Carolinians in general are Vile and Corrupt. The whole country is in a state of Debauchery, Dissoluteness and Corruption. And how can it be otherwise? The people are composed of the outcasts of all the other Colonies who take refuge there. The civil police is hardly yet established. Polygamy is very common, Celibacy much more, Bastardy, no disrepute, Concubinage, general."

Much of the trouble in North Carolina stemmed from frustration over civil law. The settlers in the central and western parts of the state complained they were exploited by a bureaucracy controlled by the rich traders of the coastal area. Taxes were high and fees extortionate. A marriage license cost $15 — more money than the average man saw in a year — and to get it one might have to travel a hundred miles. Consequently, many residents of faraway places simply took each other before God and their neighbors and considered themselves married. Descendants of William Lenoir, the patrician of Happy Valley, have searched for a century for evidence of his marriage to Ann Ballard. No records have been found, but the house he built for her at Fort Defiance stands today as a monument to a shared love.

Payment of taxes was difficult because of the shortage of currency. A farmer might receive two hundred shillings for the forty bushels of wheat he carried to Cross Creek, but of the total he would receive only forty shillings in cash. The rest would be paid in salt or some other commodity. Yet when tax time came he had to pay in cash or in the sweat of his body on whatever public project a corrupt sheriff was sponsoring. So great was the corruption that in 1766 a royal governor, William Tryon, declared that "the sheriffs have embezzled more than half the public money ordered to be raised and collected by them." Yet the governor seemed unable to do much about the problem.

Eventually, citizens decided to act for themselves. Groups called "Regulators" were organized — something on the order of latter-day vigilante bands. By 1768, Regulator activity in Hillsborough brought rebellion. Regulators, incensed by the abuses of Edmund Fanning, clerk of superior court, collected by the hundreds. Governor Tryon put sixteen hundred men in the field to oppose them. A compromise resulted with Tryon promising reforms and the Regulators agreeing to pay their taxes.

Two years later there was another outbreak. Regulators invaded the Hillsborough courtroom of Judge Richard Henderson, a man of vast ambition and personal courage. They demanded that cases of several colleagues be called and dismissed. Henderson refused, adjourned court, and rode away. The Regulators took over his courtroom, appointed their own judge, and conducted their own trials. They also composed and sang a ballad about Fanning and his "civil robberies" which, so said the song, had enabled him to "lace his coat with gold."

Governor Tryon collected an army of some one thousand men, and marched against the Regulators. The Battle of Alamance near the present city of Burlington followed, but it wasn't much of a conflict. Far from being "the advance guard of the Revolution," as some writers have declared, the Regulators were simply farmers who yet were intelligent enough to know they couldn't obtain relief by armed rebellion against an empire. Only nine men were killed on each side before the Regulators departed the field. Tryon hanged a few leaders and offered pardons to the rest if they would take an oath of allegiance to the King. Within a few weeks, an estimated six thousand men took the oath. The British were left with some misconceptions about Americans' will to fight.

Tradition has it that some fifteen hundred ex-Regulators refused to take the oath and crossed the Blue Ridge to settle on the western waters. From there, the story goes, they continued their battle against government tyranny.

It is a spirited legend but little more. Most of the Regulators stayed at home, and when rebellion on a grand scale broke out four years later, they became Tories. Of the thousands who took the oath after Alamance, only 289 have been identified as active Whigs. The Provincial Congress of North Carolina appointed a committee to court the ex-Regulators and the Continental Congress voted to send two Presbyterian ministers to persuade them their oaths weren't binding. Neither effort achieved much.

It was largely because so many in the state remained loyal to the Crown, that the Revolution in North Carolina took the characteristics of civil war. Brother fought brother, neighbor fought neighbor. Few could be neutral.

As to the westward march, that was underway before Alamance. Judge Henderson helped. Eager to tap the unlimited resources beyond the mountains, he financed an expedition by Daniel Boone and John Finley in 1769. Finley, a fur trapper, had been there before and his tall tales captivated both Boone and the judge. It was decided they would follow the famous "Warrior's Path," the route used by Cherokee war parties going north to fight the Shawnees beyond the Ohio River. Two years were spent in the forbidden land. On several occasions Boone and Finley were stopped by Indians, who confiscated their illegal furs and warned them to go home and stay there. Eventually they obeyed, returning with little loot but with marvelous tales to whet the imaginations of Henderson and his financial allies. The big money was to be made in the sale of land, all agreed. Of course, with both the King and the Cherokees guarding the passes, land would be hard to sell. Something would have to happen first.

Something happened.

2

The Watauga River rises on that high plateau to which Bishop Spangenberg climbed, and flows northwestward off the plateau, its gorges broadening into a wide valley as it drops some 1,752 feet to reach Sycamore Shoals near the present town of

Elizabethton, Tennessee. Andrew Greer built a cabin in that valley about 1766. A handful of others followed, among them James Robertson in 1770.

Robertson was then living in North Carolina where he was acquainted with Judge Henderson. Newly married, he was a handsome man with blue eyes and dark hair. A natural leader, he wanted lots of land. Evidence indicates that Henderson financed his first journey to Watauga even as he took care of Boone and Finley. The settlers were planting corn when Robertson arrived, so he put in a crop and stayed around to harvest it. Then he went home to get his wife. It wasn't an easy trip. Robertson became as lost as had Bishop Spangenberg and exhausted his supplies before being rescued by two wanderers. Losing one's way was no disgrace in those trackless wilds — even Boone confessed to being "bewildered" for as long as three days. The early explorers often "blazed a trail," literally, cutting marks on trees, known as "blazes," to show the best route.

In the spring of '71, Robertson led his wife and sixteen other families back over the hills to the little community on the Watauga. On an island in the river he built the largest house yet erected west of the Blue Ridge — notice to all that he had come to stay. Clearly, Robertson was a man to watch, and soon he proved he had ability to match his ambition. He negotiated a ten year lease with the Cherokees for the land on the Watauga and the adjoining Nolichucky. The Indians later grumbled they had little choice since the settlers warned "they would stay on the land anyway."

Having given some semblance of legality to their trespass, and secured some safety from external enemies, the Wataugans decided to achieve some domestic tranquillity. Since, under the King's edict, neither the provinces of Virginia or North Carolina could annex them, they created their own government — the Watauga Association.

Lord Dunmore, royal governor of Virginia, was astonished. In his official report to London he observed that the settlers had "to all intents and purposes erected themselves into, though inconsiderable, yet a separate state." Theodore Roosevelt in his classic study, *The Winning of the West,* agreed. "They formed a written constitution," he wrote, "the first ever adopted west of the mountains or by a community composed of American-born free men . . . They were the first to do what the whole nation has since done."

While Robertson and his associates were trying to nail down what they had seized, the wily Judge Henderson financed another Daniel Boone expedition to the lands beyond the Cumberland Gap and thus touched off an Indian war. Boone went not to hunt or explore this trip. With him went his family and forty neighbors from the Yadkin. A Shawnee war party met the prisoners on the eastern side of Cumberland and opened fire. Among those killed was Boone's son, James. The rest retreated. Other incidents contributed to the growing tension over a wide area. War seemed inevitable. The settlers grabbed their rifles and mustered under their natural leaders. Little help could be expected from the colonies, who were on the eve of revolt against the British. Indeed, some patriots considered the whole affair a Royalist plot by Lord Dunmore to divert Americans from their quarrel with King George. They called it "Lord Dunmore's War" and wanted nothing to do with it. The only will to fight belonged to the frontiersmen.

. Chief Cornstalk led the Shawnees and had his troubles too. The Cherokees refused to cooperate as the settlers put together an army and rendezvoused September 7, 1774, at Greenbriar. Among the officers were such future famous names as Evan and Isaac Shelby, John and Valentine Sevier, William Christian, and James Robertson. Andrew Lewis was in command. The battle of Point Pleasant at the junction of the Kanawha — as the New River was called in those parts — and the Ohio, took place on October 10. It was a brutal struggle of equals, but it ended in defeat for Cornstalk, who had failed to destroy a divided enemy. The treaty that followed gave to the white man the land south and east of the Ohio — at least as far as the Shawnees were concerned. The Cherokee rights to the area were then obtained by

13

purchase. Boone, acting for Henderson, offered ten thousand pounds of beads, clothing, axes, knives, pots and other goods. Sycamore Shoals on the Watauga was the site of the big pow-wow which took place on March 15, 1775. Only Tsugunsini, known to whites as Dragging Canoe, spoke in opposition. His face, spotted by smallpox scars, was grim and his words were heavy as he declared:

> "Whole nations have melted away like balls of snow before the sun. The whites have passed the mountains and settled upon Cherokee lands. New cessions will be required, and the small remnant of my people will be compelled to seek a new retreat in some far distant wilderness. When the whites are unable to point out any farther retreat for the miserable Cherokees, they will proclaim the extinction of the whole race. Should we not therefore run all risks, and incur all consequences, rather than submit to further laceration of our country? Such treaties may be all right for men too old to hunt or fight. As for me, I have my young warriors about me. We will have our lands."

One week later and only a few hundred miles away, Patrick Henry would shout: "Give me liberty or give me death." Many of the white men at Sycamore Shoals would be moved by that sentiment when they heard of it, but Dragging Canoe's eloquence left them cold. Nor was his speech remembered in 1838, when most of the remaining Cherokees were rounded up and taken along "the trail of tears" to new homes in Oklahoma.

So unmoved was Daniel Boone that he left to assemble a party of axemen before the sale was completed. Dragging Canoe had a final word for him: "You have bought a fair land but there is a cloud hanging over it," said the son of Attakullaculla. "You will find its settlement dark and bloody." A few weeks later the town of Boonesborough was founded.

Business did not end for the Cherokees. Robertson, who had

found an ally in John Sevier, put forth a new proposal to buy the Watauga land previously leased. The Indians agreed to sell for two thousand pounds' worth of goods. Henderson and Sevier supplied it.

Already a legend along the frontier, Sevier was of French Huguenot descent. Relatively well educated and a captain in the Virginia line, the tall, fair-skinned, blue-eyed pioneer would one day be called the "most handsome man in Tennessee." He had married at seventeen and now, at thirty, was several times a father. Isaac Shelby had taken him to Sycamore Shoals in 1772, and he had vowed to return. The conclave with the Indians was the opportunity he had wanted. Eventually he would make his home on the Nolichucky and become "Chucky Jack" to the men of the western waters. Something of what today might be termed an "operator," he was just what the frontier needed.

A month after the bargaining session on the River of Broken Waters, the battle of Lexington was fought. On June 15, 1775, George Washington was named commander in chief and the Revolutionary War was a reality. Sevier, who knew Washington, was quick to take advantage of the developing situation. The Watauga Settlement was renamed the "Washington District of North Carolina." A year later when word of the Declaration of Independence reached the mountains, Sevier drew up an elaborate petition to the North Carolina legislature. It traced the history of the settlement and formally requested that Washington District be annexed. In return, the petition promised that "we shall adhere strictly to your determinations, and that nothing will be lacking or any thing neglected that may add weight in the civil or military establishments to the glorious cause in which we are now struggling . . ."

It's possible the promise to "add weight" militarily may have caused a smile or two when received by state officials on August 22, 1776. Yet the men making that promise meant it, and their weight was decisive at King's Mountain some four years later. Of the 110 signatures on the document, only two were represented by the "X" of the illiterate.

When the next Provincial Congress assembled at Halifax on November 12, 1776, Sevier, Robertson, John Haile and John Carter were seated as "delegates from Washington District, Watauga Settlement." They helped frame a State Constitution and a Bill of Rights. The congress also extended the state's boundary "so far as is mentioned in the charter of King Charles the Second to the late Proprietors of Carolina"— the Pacific Ocean.

Thus was the legal status of Watauga secured at last. Robertson would soon leave the area to form a settlement on Henderson-claimed land along the Cumberland, but his cousin, Charles Robertson, would remain. So would Sevier and, a few miles away, Isaac Shelby. The state opened a land office at Sycamore Shoals and the rush began. More and more people on both sides of the mountain sang this variant of a familiar Irish tune:

> Rise you up, my dearest dear
> and present to me your hand
> And we'll take a social walk
> to a far and distant land
> Where the Hawk shot the Buzzard
> and the Buzzard shot the Crow
> We'll rally in the cane-brake
> and shoot the Buffalo

3

Benjamin Cleveland was, at heart, a romantic whose most cherished possession, until he brought home a snare drum from King's Mountain, was a book of doubtful integrity. Entitled *The Life and Adventures of Mr. Cromwell, Natural Son of Oliver Cromwell,* the book was an international best-seller in 1731. Its author claimed his father was the Lord Protector of England and his mother was Elizabeth Cleveland, a former mistress of the beheaded King Charles I. If half the adventures related are true, Mr. Cromwell had an exciting life and fathered plenty of natural sons of his own. Benjamin claimed to be descended from this Cleveland-Cromwell. In their way, Benjamin's adventures were just as remarkable as those his ancestor wrote about.

Born in 1738 at an anonymous little Virginia creek called Bull Run, Benjamin moved with his family to the vicinity of Charlottesville and the mountains. He devoted his youth to fur trapping, and became famous as a brawler and gambler. In Mary Graves, daughter of a wealthy farmer, he found a wife who could help him "get above his raising." It took some doing. He was thirty-one before moving to the Yadkin River near the present town of Ronda. There, in a bend of the river, he built a huge house which still stands. It was called Round-About, drawing its name from the movement of the water around it. As the years passed and Cleveland's weight soared to three hundred pounds, the name of the house was applied to its owner — in good fun, of course.

Daniel Boone was a neighbor, and the two hunted up Roaring River and Elk Creek. Boone's tales of "Caintuck" aroused Cleveland's interest, and in the summer of 1772 he set out to see for himself. The party reached the Cumberland Gap without incident, but shortly thereafter they were accosted by a hunting party of Cherokees who reminded them they were trespassing. The visitors were deprived of their horses, their guns, and their shoes.

Cleveland asked the name and address of the Indian leader and promised to look him up if he got home safely. Mockingly, the Indian presented him with a badly battered rifle and two charges of powder and shot to help him get home safely. It was a difficult journey. The men were reduced to eating their hunting dog before making it to the Yadkin. But after a few hearty meals, Cleveland headed out again for the Cherokee towns of north Georgia to hunt for his horses. Aided by Big Bear, a chief whose size matched Cleveland, the angry hunter did recover his horses. The Indians were so impressed they gave him a large honor guard when the time came to leave. On his way home, Cleveland detoured by the Tugalo River area in western South Carolina. When the Yadkin became crowded, he decided, he would settle there.

For frontier people, a fatalistic philosophy of what will be, will be, was almost necessary. Once on the trail Cleveland and a companion stopped to eat. The companion prepared the meal as Cleveland stretched out his huge body on the ground. Looking up, he noted a large, splintered limb dangling above him. The companion voiced the belief that since it had obviously been hanging for some time, it would continue to hang. But Cleveland moved anyway. Moments later the limb broke free and fell. When the friend congratulated Cleveland on his narrow escape, the recumbent hunter replied:

"I always told you that no man would die until his appointed time."

A natural leader, Cleveland bulked large in the thinly populated areas of the upper Yadkin. The only church for forty miles was at Mulberry Fields, the present site of Wilkesboro, where the river emerges from the foothills and begans to spread. Baptists built the church but religious sects of all persuasion used it. Men attended in hunting shirts of tow linen and short breeches, leggings and moccasins. Women wore "linsey" petticoats and "bed-gowns" made of calico. In summer they wore no shoes. Rather than bonnets, they borrowed their man's hat. The hair of both men and women was clubbed, although some men preferred a queue. Sunday dinner when guests were present could be sumptuous: pork, bacon, beef, bear meat and venison, and, of course, milk, butter, cheese and honey.

Most "store-bought" goods were purchased at Cross Creek (Fayetteville) at the head of the Cape Fear River, the state's only navigable outlet to the Atlantic. (Other rivers such as the Yadkin and the Catawba ran into South Carolina and then to the sea.) The Scots who settled at Cross Creek were canny traders, and many backwoodsmen returned home angry after bartering the fruits of a year's labor at Cross Creek. What's more, the Scots, for all their outlandish kilts and bagpipes, were pro-British. Even, of all people, Flora MacDonald.

Cleveland, the romantic, could appreciate the saga of Flora MacDonald. In its own way it was as inspiring as the romances of Elizabeth Cleveland. In 1746 Flora had been a bonnie lassie on the misty Isle of Skye off the Scottish coast. She rejoiced at news that Bonnie Prince Charlie, the last of the Stuarts, had rallied Scotland and was driving southward. The British couldn't stop him in the field, but they forced him to retreat to protect Scotland against a counterinvasion. Then, on a rainy day at Culloden Moor, the weary Scots were routed by the Duke of Cumberland. They named a flower after the Duke —"Stinking Billy," it was called.

The prince, still handsome at twenty-four, became a fugitive. Flora sheltered him on Skye. Legend has it she became his mistress. But after a few weeks Charlie was picked up by a French ship and taken to Europe where he became a drunken sot. Flora, on the other hand, went to the Tower of London for a time, but the King could afford to be generous and she was soon released. She returned to Skye and married her cousin, Allan MacDonald.

Times turned tough in Scotland. Grim hunger stalked the land in the wake of the political collapse. A rush to America began and a popular song was entitled: "Going to Seek a Fortune in North Carolina." The first to leave had some money, and some sense still of independence. Those who waited, however, brought with them the memory of defeat and the habit of living under royal rule. In a new world, their old chains felt comfortable.

Flora and Allan came in 1774, bringing with them fourteen indentured servants and crates of silver plate, books, and satin bedcovers. Instantly they were accepted as community leaders. Flora, who as a girl had been a symbol of loyalty to one prince, now as a matron came to represent a similar loyalty to another. As far as Ben Cleveland was concerned, one lost cause deserved another. It might not have been a lost cause, however, if British timing had been better. With luck, the British would have conquered North Carolina in 1776. And Flora would have been the subject of new ballads.

A complicated and far-ranging campaign was devised. Sir Henry Clinton with 1,200 men was to sail from Boston to Cape Fear and there meet with a fleet carrying an army under General Cornwallis from Cork in Ireland. Royal Governor Josiah Martin, a refugee on a ship off the coast, was supposed to cause the loyal Scots to rebel and seize the docks along the Cape Fear so the British armies could land. The entrance to the river was too shallow to permit warships to come close enough to lay down a covering bombardment.

On January 10, 1776, Martin issued a proclamation calling on all loyal subjects to rally, form an army, and seize the Wilmington area at the mouth of the Cape Fear by February 25. An estimated 3,500 Scots and ex-Regulators gathered at Cross Creek. Flora MacDonald's husband was made honorary commander, but professional soldiers were in charge. Slowly the army began moving toward the coast.

The Patriots weren't idle. Various "Minute Men" units, alerted by couriers, began to gather. One of them was commanded by Ben Cleveland from the Yadkin. He moved so fast he captured such well-known Tories as Gideon Wright before they could move eastward. Overall command was held by James "Mad Jimmie" Moore, a veteran of the French and Indian War and a friend of Cleveland. By hard marching the Patriots reached Moore's Creek, which flowed into the Cape Fear about eight miles from the coast. They crossed it and prepared a trap.

The Scots, who had moved slowly, hoping for word that white sails had appeared off the coast, reached a crude bridge over the creek as dawn broke. The advance guard led by Alexander McLeod, Flora MacDonald's son-in-law, started across only to discover that most of the planks had been removed and the logs greased. From the cypress swamps on both sides of the bridge came a withering fire. McLeod died with his claymore in hand. Not a Scot got across the creek. And above and below the bridge, the Patriots waded to attack the Scots on both flanks. It was over very quickly with a loss of one dead, one wounded, for the Minute Men.

No great revenge was taken on the Scots, but Cleveland was assigned to round up some die-hard Tories who persisted in fighting. A Colonel Sutherland has been quoted as commenting: "I don't recollect, after Cleveland had done with them, to have heard much more of those wretches during the war." Flora MacDonald and her husband were jailed at Halifax and their plantation was confiscated. Flora sold her silver plate to finance their return to Scotland in 1779. They named a woman's college after her in North Carolina, and in Scotland they continued to sing:

> Flora's beauty is surprising
> Like Bright Venus in the morn . . .

A romantic story, yes, but the aftermath of the battle was not romantic.

Clinton finally arrived off Cape Fear on March 12. Cornwallis, delayed by storms, didn't arrive until May 3. Governor Martin sadly reported the premature rising of the Scots. After some weeks of hesitation, the British decided to hit Charleston, South Carolina. To prevent reinforcements from reaching that major seaport, they agreed to encourage the Cherokees to go on the warpath from Georgia to Virginia.

John Stuart, the King's Superintendent for Southern Indians, was ordered to encourage his charges "to take up arms against his majesty's Enemies and distress them in all their power." Thirty horse-loads of ammunition were delivered to the Cherokees and such chiefs as Dragging Canoe were eager. Others hesitated, however, and entered into negotiations with the whites. The wily Sevier managed to prolong the talk period while the settlers built stockades and got ready. The delay didn't hurt the British very much, since the threat of war was enough to immobilize the frontier. Clinton proceeded to besiege Charleston.

Key to the harbor was Sullivan's Island. On it the defenders had a half-finished fort built largely of sand and palmetto roots. Colonel William Moultrie had mounted twenty-five guns in the fort, but the British might easily have sailed past unharmed. Instead, Commodore Sir Henry Parker decided to reduce it. Troops landed on nearby Long Island were supposed to wade over to Sullivan and capture it after the guns had been knocked out. Unhappily, the men discovered the gap was too deep to wade and too shallow to accommodate boats.

The real heroes of the battle were the palmetto roots. As anyone who has tried to clear them off land knows, they are practically indestructible. The cannon balls from nine warships fell like rain, and did no damage. Moultrie's men returned a deadly fire. Two of the British ships ran aground while trying to maneuver, and a third ship was burned. One blast swept the commodore's ship, killing sixty-one men and blowing off the commodore's breeches. The duel lasted until sunset. At 11 P.M. the British slipped their cables and sailed north for an assault on New York. Four years would pass before they returned.

4

Less than a week after the British were defeated at Charleston, their Indian allies struck along the frontier in coordinated attacks from northern Georgia to southern Virginia. By mid-July, hundreds of homes had been burned and every settler left alive was huddled in a stockade with his neighbors. The heaviest attack was aimed at the settlements along the Watauga, the Nolichucky and the Holston — all beyond the Proclamation Line of 1763. Nancy Ward, a cousin of Dragging Canoe, warned the settlers the attacks were coming. Half white (her father was an English officer) she bore the title *Ghigan*, the highest rank a Cherokee woman could achieve. It carried the right to speak in council like a man and to pronounce pardons. Opposed to the war on the logical grounds the Indians couldn't win, she tipped off the settlers.

The Raven led one war party against Carter Valley, a new settlement between the Clinch and Holston rivers. He met no organized resistance, the settlers having fled to less exposed communities, and he swept on into southwestern Virginia, burning and scalping.

A chief named Old Abram arrived sooner than expected at Fort Caswell, as the stockade at Sycamore Shoals was called. Some of the women were outside the walls doing the morning milking. All escaped easily except Catherine Sherill, who had wandered some distance in search of a stray cow. "Bonnie Kate," as she was called, was fast on her feet, however, and she ran for the gate with an Indian in grim pursuit. The gate was closed before she got there but John Sevier — the "Beau Sabreur" of the border — shot the Indian and reached over the stockade with arms outstretched.

"Jump for me, Kate," he yelled.

The girl gave a mighty leap into Sevier's arms. Four years later on the eve of King's Mountain she married him, his first wife having died shortly before.

The siege lasted two weeks before Old Abram gave it up as a bad job and went home.

Dragging Canoe, meantime, had encountered a surprise. Leading the largest detachment against the settlements on the Holston, he was met outside the stockade by 170 whites who figured they were as good woodsmen as the Indians. The battle of Island Flats on July 20, 1776, was rather unique in that it was fought in the open woods. Dragging Canoe was wounded and carried off the field by his defeated braves. He learned a lesson. Bravery was not enough. The white man was no longer an enemy to despise.

Even before the Indian was repulsed, a counterattack was in the making. On June 14, 1776, Brigadier General Griffith Rutherford of the Salisbury District reported to his superiors:

23

I am under the Nessety of sending you by Express, the Allcrming Condition this Contry is in, the Indins is making Grate prograce in distroying & Murdering in the frunteers of this County. 37, I am informed, was killed last Wedensday and Thursday on the Cuttaba River. I am also informed that Col McDowel, 10 men & 120 women and children is Beshaged in sume kind of fort & the Indins Round them, no help to them before yesterday and they were surrounded on Wedensday. I expect the Nex account to here that all Distroyed. Pray Gentelmen Consider oure Distress. send us Plenty of Powder & I hope under God we of Salisbery District is able to stand them, but, if you allow us to go to the Nation, I expect you will order Hilisborough District to joyn Salisbery. Three of oure Captains is kiled & one wounded. This day I set out with what men I can Raise for the Relefe of the Distrest.

Rutherford was described by his contemporaries as "uncultivated in mind or manners, but brave, ardent and patriotic." His reference to being allowed "to go to the Nation" meant carrying the war to the Cherokee Nation. And that is what was done.

A three-pronged drive began in August. South Carolina troops under Colonel Andrew Williamson drove up into the Great Smokies from the south. Virginians under Colonel William Christian pressed down the Blue Ridge from the north. And Rutherford, with the largest force, hit the center. Some 5,300 men were involved in the combined effort.

Among the "chosen Rifle Men" who rendezvoused with Rutherford at Cathey's Fort on the headwaters of the Catawba was a regiment from Surrey County. Junior officers included Captain Ben Cleveland, just back from Moore's Creek Bridge, and Lieutenant William Lenoir. It is with Lenoir that we now concern ourselves.

Like Sevier, of French Huguenot descent, Lenoir was born in Virginia in 1751. The father died shortly after moving his family to Halifax, North Carolina. Somehow, the boy got a smattering of education, and in 1771 he opened a "reading school." Two of his students were named Ballard. Their father was considered wealthy and they had a pretty sister, Ann. She was twenty, and tired of waiting for a suitable suitor. Lenoir was equally ready for marriage. When the father objected, the couple eloped. When they returned home they said they were married. Perhaps. No record has been found. In any case, Lenoir set out to improve his status. He became a surveyor and began dabbling in land. Soon he took his wife to the Yadkin Valley and settled on Fishing Creek, about four miles east of the present city of Wilkesboro. There he was more or less adopted by Benjamin Cleveland. Their friendship never wavered in years to come for, despite superficial differences, they were much alike in their romantic approach to women, to liberty, and to land.

Lenoir organized a company of Minute Men. Later he commanded "Lenoir's Rangers." In the early summer of 1776 he was busy chasing Indians from the Yadkin to New River, returning home just in time to join with Cleveland in Rutherford's expedition. Some thirty-nine years later, he looked back on that affair and wrote:

> I believe our whole number was between two and three thousand, with a small supply of ammunition and provisions. I believe the Gen'l himself was without a tent. A few officers and men had something like a wagon cover stretched to shelter them from the rain. There were very few imported blankets in camp, and at that time there was not a store within 45 miles of Fort Defiance, and very few sheep in this newly settled country and no attempt to raise cotton. Our sole means of procuring clothing were of hemp, flax and tow. Our blankets were usually made of the same materials. When striped, they were called Linsey blankets.

At that time if a gentleman could procure a hunting shirt made of good tow linen and died [sic] black, with a motto across the breast in large white letters, "LIBERTY OR DEATH," and a pair of stout breeches and leggins of the same texture, and a buck's tail on his wool hat for a cockade, he was fine enough for anything. In fact, our good Gen'l's hunting shirt was inferior — a dingy colored, ordinary looking one. We had no Government to provide for us, it being before our State Constitution was formed.

Lenoir, a very careful observer, kept a "Memorandum Book" for most of his adult life, and in it he recorded a running account of Rutherford's campaign. His 1835 account was based on that record and differs only in the fact that his spelling had improved. He told of climbing the Blue Ridge from the head of the Catawba where Old Fort now stands to Swannanoa Gap near the present site of Asheville. They then moved westward past Waynesville to the Cherokee towns along the Tennessee River.

No quarter was given despite little resistance. All towns were burned and all cornfields destroyed. The South Carolina troops driving up the mountains under Williamson were even more ruthless — their General Assembly had promised to pay a bounty of seventy-five pounds for each Indian scalp. The South Carolina men earned their pay, however, falling into an ambush in Noewee Pass. Seventeen men were killed and twenty-nine wounded before the army broke through. Lenoir, passing in the vicinity of the battlefield a few days later, reported seeing "the Dead Indians lying & where they buried their dead in a Branch and made a Cosey over them."

From the north came Christian's army, burning towns and rescuing white settlers as it marched. The Indians, overwhelmed by this example of massive retaliation, fled deeper into the mountains. Dragging Canoe retreated to an inaccessible refuge on Chickamauga Creek, in what is now Tennessee.

Rutherford's men endured great handicaps in the campaign

and their return was hampered by heavy rains. "Horses would slip sometimes 20 or 30 feet," Lenoir reported. By October 4 they neared Crider's Fort, now the site of Lenoir High School, and the young note-taker scribbled in his book:

"Capt. Cleveland & I treated the men with 2 gallons of Brandy & and at Crider's fort he treated with 7 or 8 Galns of cyder. I got home Monday nt. 7 Oct. 1776."

The following year, Cleveland and Lenoir took their troops over the mountains to Sycamore Shoals to provide protection to the settlements of Watauga Country while a treaty was being "talked" with the Cherokees. A member of the North Carolina delegation was Major Joseph Winston, under whom Lenoir would fight at King's Mountain. The treaty was signed on July 20, 1777, the first anniversary of the Battle of Island Flats.

The Indian threat to the frontier was over for the time being. The British had also abandoned their plans of conquest in the south. But the dual danger would return, greater than ever, and when it did the men on both sides of the blue mountains would rally in the canebrake and march again together.

2

The Assyrian Came Down

"We had not lain long when a rebel officer, remarkable by a hussar dress, passed toward our army within a hundred yards of my right flank, not perceiving us. He was followed by another dressed in dark green or blue, mounted on a bay horse, with a remarkably large cocked hat.

"I ordered three good shots to steal near to them and fire at them; but the idea disgusted me. I recalled the order.

"The hussar in returning made a circuit, but the other passed again within a hundred yards of us, upon which I advanced from the wood toward him. On my calling, he stopped; but, after looking at me, proceeded. I again drew his attention, and made signs to him to stop, but he slowly continued his way. As I was within that distance at which, in the quickest firing, I could have lodged half-a-dozen of balls in or about him before he was out of my reach — I had only to determine; but it was not pleasant to fire at the back of an unoffending individual who was acquitting himself very coolly of his duty; so I let him alone.

"The day after I had been telling this story to some wounded officers who lay in the same room with me, when one of our surgeons who had been dressing the wounded rebel officers, came in and told us they had been informing him that General Washington was all the morning with the light troops and only attended by a French officer in hussar dress, he himself dressed and mounted in every point as above described.

"I am not sorry that I did not know at the time who it was. Farther this deponent sayeth not, as his bones were broken a few minutes after."

So wrote Captain Patrick Ferguson to a friend in Scotland shortly after the Battle of Brandywine on September 11, 1777. Had he used his newly invented breechloading rifle against Washington, the history of the Revolution and of the United States would have been quite different. His defeat three years later at King's Mountain turned the tide of war against the British.

Pride was a decisive factor in both episodes. It would not let Ferguson shoot a fellow officer in the back at Brandywine, and it would not let him flee from "a set of mongrels" at King's Mountain. Truly, those who believe themselves to be gentlemen assume tremendous responsibilities, usually without being aware of them.

Born in 1744, Ferguson was the second son of James Ferguson of Pitfours, Aberdeenshire, Scotland. The father was a senator of the College of Justice and one of the lords commissioners of justiciary for Scotland. The mother, Anne, was the daughter of Alexander Murray, fourth lord Elibank. He was named for his uncle, Patrick Murray, a noted author. Another uncle, Brigadier-General James Murray, shaped his career. Writing from Quebec on October 11, 1759, the man who had succeeded Wolfe on the Plains of Abraham commented:

"I left orders to send Patty Ferguson to the academy at Wolich. I hope it was done. I mean to push him in my own profession."

At the time this letter was written, young Ferguson, fifteen, had already graduated from the academy and held a commission (purchased for him according to the custom of the day) as cornet in an outfit of dragoons known as the Scot Greys. A year later he was fighting the French in Germany. At one point he and a friend ventured too far from their lines and were pursued by enemy hussars. Ferguson's horse leaped a ditch. The youth, noting that one of his pistols had fallen into the ditch, wheeled the horse around and went back to get it. The enemy troops halted in astonishment, and he retrieved his weapon without incident.

Becoming ill, Ferguson was transferred back to England, where he remained until 1768, when he was sent to the British West Indies to repress a native uprising on the island of Tobago. Again his health bothered him and, after a short visit to the mainland, he returned to England in 1774.

Short and slender, possessed of large, somber eyes which stared out of a lean, almost hungry, face, Patrick Ferguson was attractive to women. But there was something about him, some quality of intensity, that discouraged a lasting alliance. He expected to achieve his ambition on the battlefield, not in the bedroom. Long after his death an English poet wrote of him:

> His heart no selfish passion ever felt,
> For there the chastest love of glory dwelt

While in America he had heard much of the vaunted skill of backwoods riflemen. Now, with rumors of rebellion rife, he undertook to devise a weapon which would put the British soldier on equal terms with the potential foe. In a patent granted by the British Patent Office on December 2, 1776, Ferguson described his weapon as "an arm which united expedition, safety, and facility in using, with the greatest certainty in execution." Its chief feature was a screw-plug attached to the trigger guard which passed through the breech of the barrel from the bottom to the top. With one turn of the trigger guard, the cham-

31

ber to the barrel could be opened or closed, allowing the shooter to insert powder and ball in an instant. It also boasted a sight capable of being elevated according to the range. The rifle was fifty inches long and weighed seven and one-half pounds. The bayonet was twenty-five inches long and one and one-half inches wide, a so-called "sword-blade bayonet" capable of taking a razor edge and being used as a short sword.

Tests of the "Ferguson Rifle" were made at Woolwich Arsenal in the summer of 1776, and before King George at Windsor. In its inventor's hands it did four things never done before: it fired four shots a minute for five minutes at a target two hundred yards away; it fired six shots in one minute; it fired four shots while being carried forward at four miles an hour; and it fired after water had been poured into the barrel. What's more, Ferguson proved he could load and fire from a prone position, something impossible with the other weapons of the day. Moreover, he did all these things with an accuracy seldom achieved by any marksman.

The rifle, in short, was revolutionary — and that was its problem. It was simply too much of a departure for the conservative military mind to accept. (Almost ninety years later, United States generals opposed the introduction of breechloaders during the Civil War.) The British perhaps recognized that such a really new weapon would force them to adopt new battlefield tactics and thus perhaps bring about a reorganization of the British army. Such a change would imperil jobs, alter the status quo. But, it seemed, the rifle's impressive performance, and Ferguson's impressive relatives, couldn't be completely ignored. Orders were given to manufacture a number of the weapons, and Ferguson was sent back to America with permission to form a corps of volunteer riflemen to be equipped with the new rifle. The official purpose was, of course, to field-test the rifle, but in reality it was but a means of passing the buck.

The Battle of Brandywine was the first chance for Ferguson to prove the value of his rifle and his riflemen. Except for his failure to shoot down George Washington, he made the most of his opportunity. He was assigned to cover the approach of the British forces to Chadd's Ford as Washington tried desperately to halt General Howe's advance on Philadelphia. The riflemen did their job well, able as they were to load and fire without exposing themselves to return fire. Only two of their number were wounded, neither fatally. Unfortunately, one of the wounded was Ferguson. A bullet shattered the elbow of his right arm and it was thought for a time that it would have to be amputated. While this was avoided, the elbow was left unbending as if in a permanent if invisible sling. Later, Ferguson trained his left hand to the use of the pen and the sword, and he eventually attained a high degree of skill in both arts.

Nor was the wound the worst thing to befall Ferguson. Sir William Howe, a proud and stubborn man, had not been pleased to have Ferguson's rifle and Ferguson's riflemen thrust upon him since his advice and consent as commander in chief in America had not been sought. The wounding of Ferguson gave him his chance to act with a seeming logic. To the wounded man in the hospital, he wrote a letter praising "your gallant and spirited behaviour in the engagement of the 11th." Then he added the bad news, informing Ferguson that he considered it "proper to incorporate the rifle corps into the light companies of the respective regiments." The rifles themselves Howe didn't mention, but they went into storage and thus into limbo. No longer would they compete with Brown Bess, the British army's standard musket since 1702. After all, it had been introduced by John Churchill, Duke of Marlborough, and what was good enough for the duke was good enough for Sir William, who had a reputation for liking both ladies and leisure. Indeed, one English wit wrote a little verse:

> Awake, arouse Sir Billy
> There's forage in the plain
> Leave your little filly
> And open the campaign

While Ferguson was recovering from his wound, Howe was replaced as supreme commander, but his order still stood. Disgusted, but a true soldier, the young Scot resumed his duties in time to take part in the Battle of Monmouth on June 28, 1778.

The war to this date had been a stalemate with leadership on both sides more concerned with *not losing* than with winning. Cities were taken and surrendered as if a game were being played, but neither side was willing to risk its army to destroy the other. The strategy in both camps was to wear each other out rather than to win decisively in the field. Certainly, the generals confronting each other weren't Napoleons, and their defects were exaggerated by caution deriving from the very nature of the conflict.

When the war started there were an estimated 700,000 men of fighting age in the thirteen colonies. Had ten percent of these potential soldiers been willing to submit to discipline for the sake of liberty, the war could have been quickly won. The British, rather obviously, would have been overwhelmed. Yet at war's end, Washington had barely nine thousand men under arms. There were almost that many Tories in British uniforms. Had the British regarded the struggle as a civil conflict instead of a rebellion, the Tories might have won the war for them. It boiled down to an ironic situation that had the British leaders failing to trust their Loyalist allies, while the Patriot rank and file didn't trust their leaders.

George Washington's big problem was his desire to be a conventional commander of armies when no such armies existed. His prior military training had been in the French and Indian War under Braddock and his successors. Douglas Southall Freeman, a biographer of Washington, noted that at the end of that war Washington "had learned scarcely anything about the utilization of militia and apparently he never made any allowance for their ignorance and their lack of weapons the law unreasonably expected them to provide. Their reluctance to serve, their readiness to desert, and the cowardice that many of them exhibited in the presence of the enemy created early in Washington's mind a disgust that soon became a prejudice. He had to call on them frequently but he never did so with any confidence . . . Whatever the future might hold, then, Washington would have no faith in the militia."

His lack of confidence was shared by the professional soldiers on both sides. Usually, thanks as much to inept leadership and lack of empathy, the militia justified the contempt in which it was held. But it need not have been that way as Daniel Morgan, a soldier's soldier, demonstrated at Cowpens.

Without any question, George Washington held the country together and defeated the British hope of victory by so doing. But he didn't win the war in a military sense and, at the end, the help of the citizen-soldier was decisive.

The Battle of Monmouth closed the first long phase of the conflict. Sir Henry Clinton, now a knight of the Bath, had succeeded Howe. His secret orders signed by the King required him to assume the defensive in the North while mounting an attack in the South. He was authorized to abandon Philadelphia, and promptly did so. It was on his retreat from that city with some ten thousand men that he encountered Washington at Monmouth. This sharp fight was the last important engagement in the North and the last fought by Washington until the siege of Yorktown more than three years later. Appropriately enough, it was a draw. Clinton continued his retreat unhindered.

The opening gun of the new war was fired at Savannah, Georgia, where on December 29, 1778, a sea-borne army of 3,500 men captured the town. It was the first major action in the South since the abortive attack on Charleston in 1776, and was, of course, the prelude to a new attack on that important port. Ironically, this new use by the British of their fleet to move men and supplies vast distances didn't begin until their naval superiority was threatened by the entry of France into the war:

Another example of poor planning in London where a succession of mediocre cabinet officers pulled strings three thousand miles long.

The development of the new strategy was delayed through 1779 by the failure of those London officials to send promised reinforcements and by the reappearance of a French fleet under Admiral Charles d'Estaing. An unsuccessful attempt to retake Savannah on October 9, 1779, caused some Americans to doubt the value of the French alliance, and convinced Clinton of the wisdom of his projected southern adventure. On December 26, 1779, he sailed from Sandy Hook with 8,700 troops and five thousand sailors and marines aboard ninety transports and ten warships. With him was Lord Cornwallis, nominally the second in command but carrying in his wallet a commission as a lieutenant general. Officially, the "dormant" commission was intended to permit Cornwallis to take supreme command in case something happened to Clinton, thus avoiding the dire possibility that authority might pass to the highest-ranking German officer, one Wilhelm von Knyphausen, who had been left in New York with fifteen thousand troops to keep Washington busy.

Also on board was Major Ferguson, newly promoted, unhappy about the manner in which his rifles and his corps of riflemen had been so summarily shelved, but eager for some action in the southern provinces where, reportedly, there were many loyal lads and lassies of Scot descent.

The fleet encountered bad weather from the beginning of the voyage, and off Cape Hatteras it was mauled by the worst storm in the memory of any sailor on board. One ship, the *Anna*, carrying two hundred Hessians, was blown all the way across the Atlantic and wrecked on the coasts of Cornwall. All the 396 horses in the expedition were lost as well as much powder and shot. The trick was to sail close enough to shore to avoid the north-moving Gulf Stream, yet far enough out to avoid the shoals. So badly was the fleet crippled that it sailed right on by

Charleston and put into the Savannah River to refit. The voyage from New York had taken thirty-eight days.

While at anchor near Savannah, Cornwallis persuaded Clinton to put Major General James Paterson ashore with 1,400 men to make a diversion toward Augusta. (Because of that dormant commission, Cornwallis usually could get what he wanted from the anxious Clinton.) Major Ferguson, with a detachment of rangers, and a Major Cochrane with the infantry of the British Legion, were assigned to protect the flanks.

It was the detached service Ferguson loved, but it had its dangers. Upon learning of a body of rebels at McPherson's Plantation, Ferguson moved quickly to surprise them. Arriving in the middle of the night, he discovered the enemy had gone elsewhere. Well, it was a good place to camp, so the tired soldiers settled down for a rest. Meanwhile, Cochrane, getting the same information about the rebels, made a forced march and arrived at the same plantation on the same night. Mistaking Ferguson's men for the rebels, he ordered an attack. Assuming the attackers were rebels trying to regain the plantation, Ferguson fought back. While parrying a bayonet with his sword, he received a wound in his left arm. Luckily, Cochrane realized his mistake about that point and managed to stop the battle. Ferguson, his arm dripping blood, called forward the man who had wounded him and gave him a piece of money as a reward for his aggressive spirit. Then everyone went to sleep. It had been a long day's night.

Next day Lieutenant Anthony Allaire, one of Ferguson's officers, noted in his diary:

> Remained at McPherson's plantation, living on the fat of the land, the soldiers every side of us roasting turkeys, fowls, pigs, every night in great plenty; this Mr. McPherson being a great Rebel and a man of vast property at present in Charleston.

37

Despite his doctor's fear that he would lose his left arm, Ferguson healed quickly and kept the field. Within four days he was on the march again with Allaire reporting:

> This day's march was very tedious — a disagreeable, rainy, cold day, and through a swamp where the water was from two to three feet deep.

Three days later they reached "a village containing about sixty houses, situated on the Pon Pon or Edisto river." Allaire decided: "It is a pleasant little place, and well situated for trade, but the inhabitants are all Rebels — not a man remaining in the town except two, one of whom was so sick he could not get out of bed, and the other a doctor who had the name of a friend to Government. The women were treated very tenderly, and with utmost civility, notwithstanding their husbands were out in arms against us."

But two days later, Allaire reported:

> This day Col. Ferguson get the rear guard in order to do his King and country justice by protecting friends and widows and destroying Rebel property; also to collect live stock for the use of the army, all of which we effect as we go, by destroying furniture, breaking windows, etc., taking all their horned cattle, horses, mules, sheep, fowls, etc., and their negroes to drive them.

This was the scorched earth policy which was to make Ferguson infamous and contribute greatly to anti-British feeling in the Carolinas. Some men won't fight for liberty but they will kill to save their cows, a fact a Scotsman should have known above all others. The activities of British troops and such Tory allies as "Plundering Sam Brown" and his sister, Charity, gave the Patriots excuse to retaliate on the Tories. Since, by and large, the Tories were often more prosperous, the bargain wasn't a bad one. More and more the war in the South took on the attributes of a civil conflict.

The diversion to Augusta was quickly canceled in favor of an overland drive on the main objective. Assigned to assist was Colonel Banastre "Bloody Ban" Tarleton, a dashing figure whose ruthless deeds caused even Cornwallis to remark of him: "There spoke the saber." Tarleton was young, ambitious, and a womanizer of wide reputation. On his return to England he was said to have boasted "in the presence of a lady of respectability, that he had killed more men and ravished more women than any man in America." Ferguson, who could put up with much in the name of duty, found the cocky redhead personally obnoxious and had as little to do with him as possible. One joint operation, while successful, ended in an incident that enraged Ferguson. Patriots attempting to keep Charleston's communications open to the interior were surprised at Monck's Corner in the early morning darkness of April 4, and routed. About three hundred badly needed horses were captured and other supplies as well. Tarleton's dragoons, exhilarated by the victory, began plundering nearby houses. Lieutenant Allaire confided to his diary that "three ladies came to our camp in great distress . . . They had been most shockingly abused by a plundering villain. Lady Colleton badly cut in the hand by a broadsword, and bruised very much." The "cursed villain that abused them" was caught and sent to camp where Ferguson wanted to hang him instantly, along with some other dragoons who had been overly playful. Instead, they were sent to headquarters and flogged. Allaire, meanwhile, escorted the ladies to a nearby plantation where "we bid adieu to our fair companions with great regret, they thinking themselves out of danger of any insults."

Chivalry was not yet dead in the Deep South, but for that fact Tarleton could claim no credit.

General Benjamin Lincoln, Commander of the Southern Department, led the defense of Charleston. A Massachusetts farmer who had worked his way up the militia hierarchy, Lincoln had about 3,600 men under arms when the British sails appeared off Charleston on February 10. Of these, some 1,800 were Continentals — those men who had enlisted for the duration and as a result of training and experience considered themselves to be "regulars" as opposed to the militia who signed up for thirty or ninety days and went home when their time expired. The Continentals looked askance at the militia, and sometimes with reason, but in the South, at least, the militia had by far the better record. The fact that their leaders were selected on the basis of ability rather than political influence may have had something to do with it. In March, an additional force of 1,500 Continentals drawn originally from North Carolina and Virginia fought their way in, but after the battle at Monck's Corner the gate was closed. Only a third of the defenders of Charleston were South Carolinians, a fact that tells much about the attitude of the people and the state of the fortifications. Four years of untouched prosperity had left Charleston unprepared to fight.

A crude fort in Charleston harbor had stopped the British fleet in 1776. It had been renamed Fort Moultrie in honor of its former commander, but it had been allowed to decay. Here is Lieutenant Allaire's version of its fall:

> Sunday, 7th. Orders to get ready to march with two day's provisions at a minute's notice. Maj. Ferguson had obtained permission to attack Fort Moultrie. He rode forward with four dragoons to reconnoitre. We were to remain at our posts till we got orders for marching. The first news we heard was the fort was in possession of the British; the Rebels had surrendered themselves prisoners of war. Capitulation was as follows: Capt. Hudson of the Navy summoned the fort on Friday, and received for answer: "Tol, lol, de rol, lol: Fort Moultrie will be defended to the last extremity." On Saturday he sent another flag, and demanded a surrender. At this Col. Scott changed the tune of his

> song . . . About eight o'clock Sunday morning, Colonel Scott with his men, about one hundred and twenty, marched out of the fort, piled their arms. Capt. Hudson marched in, took possession of Fort Moultrie, the key to Charleston harbor; which puts it in our power to keep out any forcing enemy that would wish to give the Rebels any assistance . . .

General Lincoln has been much criticized for failing to withdraw his troops after it became apparent he couldn't hold the city. The record shows that when he proposed withdrawal in April, the citizenry threatened to join the British and attack the withdrawing Continentals. By May 11, however, after the fall of Fort Moultrie, the city officials were demanding surrender on any terms to stop the bombardment which threatened to burn the town. Clinton demanded unconditional capitulation. After thinking about it one day, Lincoln agreed. Allaire put it this way:

> Friday 12th. The gates were opened. Gen. Leslie at the head of the British Grenadiers, Seventh, Sixty-third and Sixty-fourth regiments, and Hession Grenadiers marched in, and took possession of Charleston, and soon leveled the thirteen stripes with the dust and displayed the British standard on their ramparts.

Six thousand men — the entire Continental military establishment in the South — were lost, along with a vast supply of powder and shot, muskets and other supplies. The best port south of Philadelphia was in British hands. The shock to morale was beyond measure. The darkest hour was approaching and for many the war was all but over.

Some forty miles from Charleston about 350 men, comprising the 3rd Virginia Continentals, got news of the surrender and made an about-face. Colonel Abraham Buford realized that trained soldiers in the South were as rare as hen's teeth and

41

more precious than diamonds, so he started his men back to North Carolina as fast as they could march. Unfortunately, Tarleton could ride faster. Lord Cornwallis, preparing to take over from Clinton as field commander, ordered "Bloody Ban" after the retreating Rebels, with some 270 men. Horses dropped dead along the road, but Tarleton's men stole new ones and kept going. They covered 105 miles in fifty-four hours when on the afternoon of May 29, they caught up with Buford near the North Carolina line.

Under a flag of truce, Tarleton demanded surrender. He had seven hundred men in hand, he said, and Lord Cornwallis was a few hours behind with nine battalions. The Rebels had no chance.

Buford obviously didn't believe Tarleton, and formed his men for battle. Instantly, without waiting to bring up his stragglers, Tarleton ordered a charge. The Continentals held their ground although none had experienced a cavalry charge before. Buford, however, ordered them to hold their fire until the enemy was within a hundred feet. This was too close to stop cavalry, leaving no time to reload and fire a second volley.

In seconds the dragoons were among the footmen, slashing with their sabers. Infantrymen, who had ridden double behind the dragoons to reach the field, followed up with a bayonet charge. The battle became a slaughter. An officer tried to raise a white flag and Tarleton in person cut him down.

Someone killed Tarleton's horse and, according to Tarleton, "a report amongst the cavalry that they had lost their commanding officer . . . stimulated the soldiers to a vindictive asperity not easily restrained. Upwards of one hundred officers and men were killed on the spot."

The Americans complained that not only did Tarleton's men ignore a call for quarter, but, after the battle had ended, "went over the ground plunging their bayonets into everyone that exhibited any signs of life." Captain John Stokes was said to have received 23 wounds, including a saber cut that took off his right hand and four bayonet thrusts through the body. Somehow he lived to tell about it.

A total of 113 Virginians died in battle and 150 more were so badly wounded they were left to die. Fifty-three were captured, most of them wounded. Tarleton lost five killed, twelve wounded.

He had his victory, but the Patriots had a bitter phrase with which to taunt the Tories on other days: "Tarleton's quarter," which meant no quarter at all. And the password on King's Mountain would be "Buford."

It was still early, but already the year was beginning to take shape.

2

Lord Cornwallis might not have been in South Carolina at all had his wife, Jemima, remained in good health. He had married for love at some cost to his prestige, and had returned willingly to his wife in 1778 after having become exasperated with Sir Henry Clinton. Jemima became ill, however, and died in 1779. In an effort to ease the pain, Cornwallis turned back to the war in America.

Sir Henry, to whom Cornwallis could scarcely be polite, was also sorrowing for a woman, but she was very much alive in New York. A widower, Clinton had fallen in love with his housekeeper upon first meeting her. It was a rather interesting reaction on his part as she was with child at the time by her husband. After the baby's birth, Clinton pressed his suit and even detected some encouragement in the husband's manner. Still Mrs. O'Callaghan resisted, and it wasn't until she discovered her husband having an affair with "a common strumpet" that she came to Clinton and — his word — surrendered. Not even the fall of Charleston made him happier.

Having tasted the joys of victory, Clinton was not unhappy

when word of a new French fleet headed for America gave him an excuse to hurry back to New York. Cornwallis, who had long hungered for an independent command, was happy to see him go.

Technically, Clinton's instructions to His Lordship stressed defensive operations with the objective of holding safe for the Crown the provinces of Georgia and South Carolina. But Clinton, wittingly or otherwise, left Cornwallis a loophole by authorizing offensive operations of a defensive nature. In other words, anything that strengthened British control was permissible. Cornwallis, who believed that the best defense was an attack, construed these instructions to mean he had ample authority to advance through North Carolina into Virginia since, by doing so, he would be protecting the lower provinces.

Of course.

Cornwallis also got permission to bypass his superior in New York and communicate directly with London. Such procedure, he pointed out, would save much time. Clinton agreed. If the people in London wanted to authorize Cornwallis to make a fool of himself, it was fine with him. Hell, he'd been trying to resign for more than a year anyway.

Before departing for his housekeeper's bed, Clinton called in Major Ferguson and promoted him to Inspector-General of Militia. The assignment was basically to organize and command the Tories who, Clinton assumed, would flock to colors in increasing numbers now that the war was so obviously won. Reportedly, Clinton was warned that Ferguson was "hot-tempered," but he replied that he didn't believe malicious rumors and cited a couple about himself as proof of their unreliability.

To aid Ferguson's recruiting efforts, Clinton issued a proclamation calling on all citizens to return to their allegiance and take an active role in sustaining the royal order of things. Anyone failing to do so would be treated as a rebel.

The proclamation was a mistake. A lot of former enemies had given their parole and intended to observe neutrality. Now they were asked to join the British and fight their former friends.

A lot of men took the required oath with serious reservations, and some left home and went searching for a Rebel band to join. But even the Tories didn't like the procedure since, they said, all a notorious Whig had to do to reacquire the privileges of British citizenship was to sign a paper and salute. It didn't seem fair, somehow. Amnesty never does — to some.

Unworried was Clinton. "I leave Lord Cornwallis here with sufficient force to keep it against the world," he wrote, and sailed off to New York. The year was to prove lucky for Sir Henry. Before it ended, Mrs. O'Callaghan's husband conveniently died. Presumably he could have married his love, but that wasn't necessary, was it? The affair continued happily for some fifteen years.

Perhaps Clinton was wise in not legalizing his relationship with his housekeeper. The children of such marriages sometimes had difficulty in achieving social confidence. Take the case of Horatio Gates.

Born in 1728 to the Duke of Leeds's housekeeper, Gates seemed afflicted with an offensive personality and a desire to get ahead by any means possible. Contemporary writers called him "a snob of the first water" with "an unctuously pious way" about him. At an early age he entered the British army and was rapidly promoted. He was wounded at Monongahela. Retiring in 1765 as a major, he settled down with George Washington's help to become a gentleman farmer in Virginia. The outbreak of the Revolution gave him a major opportunity, for he recognized that the Patriots would desperately need professionally trained officers.

All went well for a time, but in 1777 he "made a spectacle of himself" on the floor of Congress by turning a promise to deliver firsthand information into a bitter attack on those who had bypassed him in giving command assignments. Shortly thereafter, Washington helped him win the job of commander of the Northern Department. He arrived just in time to be named the "Hero of Saratoga" when "Gentleman Johnnie" Burgoyne surrendered his army. The country desperately needed a hero and while there were those who felt that Daniel Morgan and Benedict Arnold deserved the credit, it was Gates who got the glory.

The worship of a victorious commander reached such heights that there was a movement launched to replace Washington with Gates. There seems no doubt that Gates cooperated with the conspiracy, but when it backfired he was still agile enough to make his peace with the patient Washington.

With the war moving south, it was necessary to appoint a commander of the Southern Department. Gates's friends in Congress were strong enough to get the job for him. Washington wasn't consulted. Gates was told to get down to South Carolina and recover that state as well as Georgia.

Up to this point Gates had been extremely lucky. Had his run of luck continued he might today be known as the hero of his country. As it was this "old granny-looking fellow," as one soldier saw him, was almost its executor. General Charles Lee, who had been sent south in 1776 — arriving too late to do any harm — told Gates on his departure to "take care lest your Northern laurels turn into Southern willows."

Pending Gates's arrival, the American army in the South — such as it was — was under the command of another foreign-born officer who pretended to be more than he was, socially speaking. But there's a monument to him today in South Carolina.

Shortly after Clinton's sails appeared off Charleston, Congress sent reinforcements marching south under the command of a professional soldier who called himself Baron de Kalb. The title was phony, for the man had been born simple Hans Kalb, but he was a solid soldier who had seen plenty of action in Europe before being commissioned a major general in America.

The march began in Morristown, Pennsylvania, on April 16 — with some two thousand soldiers, Continentals from Maryland and Delaware. They reached North Carolina before hearing on June 20th of Charleston's fall five weeks before. Kalb moved on, desperate now for provisions, and uncertain as to what he was supposed to do. A few reinforcements from militia outfits joined him, but the quartermaster organizations to the north had broken down and no supplies were coming through. Kalb pitched camp on Deep River in central North Carolina and tried to live off the country until the situation resolved itself. When official word finally came, it announced the appointment of Horatio Gates — the son of the English housekeeper.

Gates arrived in camp on July 25, and was saluted with thirteen guns. He brought no food, no fresh troops, and no doubts as to what should be done. Congress wanted action, by God, and he would give it some. He ordered the tattered army to be ready to march on a moment's notice.

Cornwallis had not been idle while Kalb's men marched south. Extending control of South Carolina, and preparing, incidentally, for the big push north, the British established a major base at Camden on that section of the Catawba River known in South Carolina as the Wateree. (A few miles south, it becomes the Santee.) Lord Francis Rawdon, a young and aggressive aide of Cornwallis, was in command. Advance posts were established at Cheraw, Hanging Rock, and Rocky Mount.

Upon taking charge, Gates found a report from General Thomas Sumter, the "Carolina Gamecock" who had won a reputation as a guerrilla, to the effect that Rawdon's strength numbered only about seven hundred men. That the report was already old did not deter Gates — immediately he decided to attack Rawdon and capture Camden. De Kalb and his officers were appalled; the men were in no condition to fight a battle. If, however, Gates was determined, why not swing west through Salisbury to the Catawba and go down it? Such a route would be through friendly country where food was plentiful.

No, said Gates. He wanted to surprise Camden, and a straight hike across the country would save fifty miles. In vain did the local men point out the area was largely barren pinelands and swamp. Gates refused to change his mind, insisting they would find corn in the valley of the lower Yadkin (called Peedee in South Carolina). They did find corn, but it was still green. The hungry soldiers ate it anyway, and it made them sick. Wearily the army of scarecrows staggered on. Gates, meanwhile, was writing dispatches about the progress of "the Grand Army of the South."

Unknown to Gates, Cornwallis established himself in Camden on August 13, taking up residence in the best house in town. The owner of the house, a Patriot, was banished to Bermuda. Having made himself comfortable, the Earl sent a spy to drop in on General Gates. Somehow, the enterprising young man succeeded. Gates granted him an interview and confided, among other things, that he had some six thousand men under arms. This was a gross exaggeration, but Gates gets no credit for misleading the enemy — he actually believed his figure was correct. Former Governor Caswell joined him with 1,200 North Carolina militia including Brigadier General Griffith Rutherford, the former scourge of the Cherokees. Other detachments came in until, on paper, the Grand Army numbered 4,100. When, however, aides pointed out that only 3,052 were present and fit for duty, Gates shrugged:

"There are enough for our purposes."

Six thousand or half that number, it really didn't matter to Cornwallis. He had only 2,239 officers and men at Camden — the rest were scattered throughout Georgia and South Carolina. However, he believed that his regulars were superior to any number of Rebels led by Gates — and in that opinion he may have been right.

The American army was dead on its feet from fatigue and starvation when, on the afternoon of August 15, Gates ordered a night march on Camden. At this late date he was still ignorant of Cornwallis's arrival there. To give his men strength for the final push, Gates provided a meal of "bread and fresh beef with a dessert of molasses mixed with mush." The effect was disastrous; the bowels of the army turned to water, leaving the men weaker than before. Gates, it would appear, was as bad a dietitian as he was a general.

At 10 P.M. the march began under a moonless sky. There was

just light enough to see the white sandy road and the outline of pine trees against the horizon. It was hot and muggy with no breeze. Constantly the men broke rank to answer the call of the molasses they had eaten. No one, except, perhaps Gates, was happy.

By coincidence, Cornwallis moved north out of Camden at exactly the same time. His goal was a surprise attack on Gates. About 2:30 A.M. the advance patrols of both armies ran into each other in the middle of Gum Swamp. There was an exchange of shots, some saber work by horsemen, and both sides pulled back to await the coming of daylight so they could discover what was going on.

Gates called his staff — which numbered eight generals — together and asked for advice. The men were almost too shocked by such condescension to reply. Only one spoke and he asked a question:

"Gentlemen, is it not too late *now* to do anything but fight?"

The pitiless sun rose upon the hapless army. Cornwallis deployed in a line perpendicular to the road, extending on both flanks to the swamps. Gates was forced to follow suit. The location of the battle was such that no wide sweeps or clever tricks were possible. It was to be a head-on conflict. Since Gates had twice as many men as Cornwallis, the advantage should have been his. But he stood waiting, apparently too stricken to give commands. A brigade of Virginians did try to attack the British right flank, but turned and fled as the mass of British regulars began moving inexorably forward with bayonets fixed. Instead of chasing the Rebels, the troops turned to hit the flank of the North Carolina militia left exposed. Panic was contagious and soon the Carolinians were running too. Rutherford was wounded and captured.

Only on the American right did Baron de Kalb and his Continentals stand firm under the repeated attacks of Lord Rawdon. Colonel Otho Williams attempted to bring the reserve to his aid, but was driven off the field by the now superior British forces. Kalb fought on alone and now Tarleton was ordered to

49

give the coup de grâce with his dragoons. Unhorsed, the soldier of fortune fought on foot until mortally wounded. Cornwallis, flushed with triumph, was yet moved enough to ride up to the fallen foe and say:

"I am sorry, sir, to see you; not sorry to see that you are vanquished, but sorry to see you so badly wounded."

What, if anything Kalb said in reply, was not recorded. He died three days later and was buried in a Camden churchyard. As far as the Americans had one, he was the hero of Camden.

And where was General Gates as the man he had replaced fell fighting on a stricken field? He was on his horse getting as far away from Camden as possible. He covered the sixty miles to Charlotte before the sun set.

Some indication of Gates's haste in departing the battlefield was noted by Major William R. Davie, who was enroute to join the Patriot army with a small troop of men. About ten miles from Camden they met a soldier in full flight. They promptly arrested him as a deserter and heard the tale of disaster. It seemed too bad to be true, but confirmation was quickly obtained. The next rider to appear was Gates himself.

The general drew rein long enough to order Davie and his men to fall back to Charlotte before Tarleton came up. Davie replied that his men were accustomed to "Bloody Ban" and did not fear him. Gates didn't stop to argue, but spurred his horse to a gallop and rode on north.

General Isaac Huger, who had some experience with Tarleton at Monck's Corner outside Charleston, came riding up. Davie asked him how far Gates's orders should now be obeyed. Huger replied:

"Just as far as you please, for you will never see him again."

Still doubtful, Davie sent a courier spurring after Gates with this question: "Shouldn't Davie go on to Camden to bury the American dead?"

He came back with this reply from Gates:

"I say retreat! Let the dead bury the dead."

And on to Charlotte went the commander of "the Grand Army

of the South." But he didn't tarry there. Two days later he had covered an additional 120 miles and reached Hillsborough in central North Carolina.

Alexander Hamilton, no friend of Gates, commented:

> Was there ever an instance of a general running away as Gates has done from his whole army? And was there ever so precipitous a flight? One hundred and eighty miles in three days and a half: It does admirable credit to the activity of a man at his time of life. But it disgraces the general and the soldier.

Gates maintained, of course, that since Hillsborough was the logical place to begin rebuilding the army, the logical thing to do was get there as quickly as possible.

"Never was a victory more complete, or a defeat more total," wrote John Marshall. It remains today one of the most disastrous defeats the American army has ever suffered. Of the four thousand men in the "Grand Army," only seven hundred eventually reached Hillsborough. Cornwallis claimed one thousand Rebels killed and eight hundred wounded — and, since Gates didn't even know how large his army was before the battle, his figures have to be accepted. What happened to the remaining 1,500, more or less, who escaped but didn't report to Hillsborough? Obviously, they had had their fill of Continental generals who fed their troops molasses instead of rum on the eve of battle.

Still, there didn't appear too much to choose from. Two days after Camden, the fire-eating Tarleton caught Sumter in the middle of a lunch break and killed 150 men. More than three hundred were taken prisoner and a hundred Tories previously captured by Sumter were freed. Sumter escaped by doing a Gates, but soon stopped running and began rebuilding.

Once again, however, the South seemed helpless at the foot of the conqueror. No Patriot force worthy of the name stood between Cornwallis and the Chesapeake. And to sweep north was his dream. Back on June 30th he had written to Clinton of his plans:

> In regard to North Carolina I have establish'd the most satisfactory correspondence, & have seen several people of credit & undoubted fidelity from that Province; They all agree in assurances of the good disposition of a considerable Body of the inhabitants, & of the impossibility of subsisting a Body of Troops in that Country until the Harvest is over. This reason, the Heat of the Summer, & the unsettled state of South Carolina, all concurr'd to convince me of the necessity of Postponing offensive operations on that side until the latter end of August or beginning of September . . . If I am not honnour'd with different directions from your Excellency before that time, I shall take my measures for beginning the execution of the above Plan about the latter end of August or beginning of September . . .

On August 6th, ten days before Camden, Cornwallis was still on schedule. He wrote to Clinton:

> The Wheat harvest in North Carolina is now over, but the weather is still excessively hot; and notwithstanding our utmost exertions, a great part of the Rum, Salt, Clothing and necessaries for the Soldiers, and the Arms for the Provincials & Ammunition for the Troops are not very far advanced on their way to Camden. However, if no material interruption happens, this business will be nearly accomplished in a fortnight or three Weeks. It may be doubted by some whether the Invasion of North Carolina may be a prudent measure, but I am convinced it is a necessary one, and that if we do not Attack that Province we must give up both South Carolina and Georgia & retire within the Walls of Charlestown . . .

> An early diversion in my favor in Chesapeak Bay will be of the greatest and most important advantage to my operations. I most earnestly hope the Admiral will be able to spare a Convoy for that purpose.

Then followed some troop dispositions in detail, and this remark:

> I shall place Ferguson's Corps & some militia of the Ninety-Six district, which Col. Balfour assures me have got into very tolerable order, owing to the great assiduity of Ferguson, on the borders of Tryon County, with directions for him to advance with part of them into the Mountains and secure the left of our March.

Following his victory at Camden, Cornwallis wasted little time. In a dispatch to Lord George Germain, the civilian in London who was supposed to be bossing the campaign, he boasted that on August 17, one day after the battle:

> I dispatched proper persons into North Carolina with directions to our friends there to take arms & assemble immediately, & seize the most Violent People and all military Stores & magazines belonging to the Rebels, & to intercept all stragglers from the routed Army; And I have promised to march without loss of time to their support. Some necessary supplies for the Army are now on their way from Charleston, and I hope that their arrival will enable me to Move in a few days.

A week and a day later he still had not moved. In a report to Clinton on August 29, he complained:

> We receive the strongest Professions of Friendship from North Carolina. Our Friends, however, do not seem inclined to rise until they see our Army in Mo-

tion. The Severity of the Rebel Government has so terrified & totally subdued the Minds of the People that it is very difficult to rouze them to any Exertions. The taking that violent and cruel Incendiary Genl. Rutherford, has been a lucky Circumstance, but the indefatigable Sumter is again in the Field, & is beating up for Recruits with the greatest assiduity . . .

In that letter, Cornwallis again mentioned his plans for Ferguson, but there was a note of doubt now:

> Ferguson is to move into Tryon County [North Carolina] with some Militia, whom he says he is sure he can depend upon for doing their Duty and fighting well; but I am sorry to say that his own Experience, as well as that of every other Officer, is totally against him.

The victorious general concluded his message to Clinton with the hope that "nothing can happen to prevent your Excellency's intended Diversion in the Chesapeak." If, he added, some "unforseen Cause should make it impossible, I should hope that you will see the absolute necessity of adding some Force to the Carolinas."

Obviously, Cornwallis was uneasy. Had he known the truth he would have been anxious. For building far to the west was a thunderhead. Out of it would come a lightning bolt.

3

A Most Horrid Conspiracy

Atop a wooded ridge overlooking the lush green of Quaker Meadows and the slow-moving Catawba River, the dead lie forgotten in an abandoned graveyard. Among them are Charles McDowell, his wife Grace, and his brother Joseph.

The McDowell brothers played key roles in the drama of 1780 that reached its climax on the crest of King's Mountain. And Grace Bowman McDowell has earned a place in legend comparable to that of "Bonnie Kate" Sevier.

Born in Virginia in 1750, Grace developed into a beautiful girl. Ordered by her father to marry a rich and elderly planter, Grace said nothing. When the ceremony began and the preacher asked the usual question:

"Do you, Grace, take this man . . .?" he got an unusual reply: "No," said Grace, "I do not."

And she didn't.

Later she married a man of her own choosing, one John Bowman, who as a captain under Colonel Charles McDowell would be fatally wounded in battle against the Tories. Grace, carrying her two-year-old daughter, rode forty miles on horseback to the battlefield, made her husband's last hours as comfortable as possible, and supervised his burial. Then she rode home. McDowell, a confirmed bachelor, was so impressed that he proposed after a decent interval. After another decent interval, she married him.

For his bride, McDowell built a mansion on the hill overlooking his plantation. The view was magnificent: to the north the wall of the Blue Ridge rising like a blow in the face; to the west and not so close, the jagged peaks of the Great Smokies, to the south, the line of foothills known locally and logically as the South Mountains.

Today, only the family cemetery and a few bricks remain. Where the house stood now stands a radio tower, broadcasting country music.

Who named Quaker Meadows seems to be a mystery. It was called that in 1752 when Bishop Spangenberg passed that way. He noted that "the land here is very rich and much frequented by buffalo whose tracks are everywhere and can often be followed with profit." The bishop was also impressed with the wolves which, he said, "give us music every morning from six corners at once, such music as I have never heard."

The McDowells came to Quaker Meadows from Winchester, Virginia, about five years after the bishop's visit. Charles, born in 1743, was thirteen years older than Joseph, and, as a result, always held higher rank although both men ended as brigadier generals in the militia. Age has also been blamed for the fact that where Charles was cautious, Joseph was aggressive. Charles liked to play the supreme commander, attending to grand strategy while other men, including his brother, fought the battles he planned. The two men seemed to have been good friends, but after Charles married, Joseph bought a farm on nearby John's River. The river, incidentally, was named for John Perkins, the guide who led Bishop Spangenberg to the top of the Blue Ridge while searching for the Yadkin.

Both brothers took part, along with Cleveland and Lenoir, in

Rutherford's epic campaign against the Cherokee towns in 1776. After that, the war settled down for a while. Charles became a colonel and Joseph a major in the interim, and both took the field shortly after the fall of Charleston on May 12, 1780.

When news of Charleston reached Quaker Meadows, Colonel McDowell mobilized his regiment and moved south to protect the borders of North Carolina. A more pressing problem, however, in view of Cornwallis's determination to wait for the harvest to be completed, were the Tories who didn't want to wait. For four years they had lain low in the expectation that eventually His Majesty's forces would return and save them from the Whigs. Now that British arms were triumphant to the south, they decided to wait no longer.

A messenger from Cornwallis arrived, wearing a tattered uniform and calling himself Lieutenant Colonel John Moore. He had gold, however, and news, and for both commodities the Tories were hungry. To make sure he was communicating, he set June 10 as the meeting date for all Tories in the area. The place was the bank of Indian Creek near the present city of Lincolnton on the Catawba in lower North Carolina. Forty men assembled, but the meeting broke up quickly as scouts brought word that Major Joseph McDowell was approaching with twenty armed men. A new date was set for June 13. The rendezvous was to be at Ramseur's Mill some seven miles away.

Some two hundred Tories showed up for the second meeting, and their numbers increased rapidly as the news spread around the countryside. In less than a week, a formidable force of some 1,300 Loyalists had assembled. Not all were armed, however — they expected King George to supply the wherewithal.

This gathering, by far the largest since the Scots rallied at Cross Creek in 1776, attracted the attention of Patriot leaders. Quickly, General Griffith Rutherford began assembling an army of militia at Charlotte. A second and much smaller assortment under Colonel Francis Locke of Rowan County came together at Mountain Creek near Moore's camp. Eventually four hundred men, including twenty-five commanded by Major McDowell, collected. The Tories were thus situated between two bodies of Patriots and in a position to destroy the smaller one before Rutherford could arrive.

Locke and McDowell took counsel. A suggestion that they try to slip around Moore's camp and join Rutherford was rejected on the grounds it would leave that area of the state at the mercy of the Tories. McDowell, always daring, then suggested they do the unexpected and attack Moore. The surprise, he thought, might more than compensate for inferior numbers.

Had a Continental officer been present, he would doubtless have dismissed the idea as too reckless, but Locke liked it. A courier was sent posthaste to Rutherford and the Patriots moved out. The column was led by three groups of mounted men; the rest followed in a double column. One historian has described the little army as "an unorganized crowd of inexperienced, undisciplined, armed civilians."

The Tories were camped on a hill about three hundred yards from Ramseur's Mill along a little road. Pickets were stationed some six hundred yards from the camp. On the approach of McDowell and his Burke County horsemen, the pickets fired once and then ran toward camp. The horsemen galloped after them, following them right into the Tory camp. Some unarmed Tories ran, but enough recovered their wits to recognize the inferior size of the attacking force. They opened fire, driving back the Burke boys. But by now the infantry was approaching. The battle became a hot affair, and a strange one. Few of the men had uniforms, and a lot of them were neighbors. The Tories looked just about like the Whigs, and it can be assumed that some men on each side were killed by mistake.

Eventually, the Tories retreated down the rear of the hill and formed a new line along its base. The Patriots tried to form along the top of the hill, but could find only eighty-six men available. After some difficulty, an additional twenty-four men were rounded up and put into position. Expresses, meanwhile, were riding to find Rutherford, who was supposed to be approaching from the north-northwest. During the lull in the battle, a flag of truce was advanced by the Patriots, officially to suggest a respite while the wounded were treated, but, in reality, to gain more time.. The Tories proved to be just as tricky, however, and while their leaders talked most of the men hightailed it for home. When the talks ended without any decision, only fifty Tories were left and they too broke and ran in a body. The Patriots were left in command of the hill. Losses on each side numbered about 20 killed and 130 wounded, but the victory against superior numbers belonged to Locke and McDowell.

Moore, the self-appointed leader of the Tories, reported to Cornwallis with only thirty men instead of the thousands he had hoped to bring. His Lordship was so angry he threatened to court-martial Moore for provoking a battle prematurely. Losing it so completely may have also been a factor in Cornwallis's rage. In a letter to Sir Henry Clinton, Cornwallis commented:

> I still hope this unlucky business will not materially affect the general Plan or occasion any commotions on the frontiers of the Province.

Lieutenant Allaire heard about it three days later and his report to his diary illustrates the manner in which a defeat is accepted and depreciated.

> Some friends came in, four wounded. The militia had embodied at Tuckasegie, on the South Fork of the Catawba river — were attacked by a party of Rebels under the command of Gen. Rutherford. The militia were scant of ammunition, which obliged them to retreat. They were obliged to swim the river at a mill dam. The Rebels fired on them and killed thirty. Col. Ferguson, with forty American Volunteers, pushed with all speed in pursuit of the Rebels. The militia are flocking to him from all parts of the country.

Despite Allaire's wishful thinking, the victory at Ramseur's Mill was a solid one. It discouraged the Tories for the second time, and made them cautious. More than an emissary from Cornwallis would be needed to get them to take arms again.

It is perhaps ironic that this little victory of "inexperienced civilians" was won on June 20, 1780, the same day that Baron de Kalb reached Hillsborough with his tattered army of Continentals. A month later he would turn that army over to Horatio Gates, who would send it staggering to its defeat at Camden.

In a well-organized war conducted according to the rules, the Continentals would have been far superior to the citizen-soldier. But the struggle in the Carolinas was essentially a civil war, and in that kind of melee the untrained civilian fighter was superior. On the whole he had much better leadership, for he exercised a veto power of a sort over his officers. If they were cowards, if they lacked imagination and dash, it was soon apparent. And having decided for one reason or another that his officers were incompetent, the citizen-soldier simply stayed home or went home when danger threatened. To die for liberty was one thing, but to die because one's neighbor was a fool or a coward was something else. The Continental, on the other hand, was a professional soldier — or the nearest thing to one on the Patriots' side. Military discipline forced him to accept a Gates or a Morgan as commander without any reservation. If the man had the rank, then discipline demanded that rank be respected. The political system being what it was, he usually got a Gates instead of a Morgan, and could consider himself lucky if a Nathaniel Greene got the nod.

Had the Continentals had proper leadership and proper numbers, they presumably could have knocked out Cornwallis in one formal battle, but, on the other hand, Cornwallis could not win no matter how many times he defeated the Continentals. His real foe was the citizen-soldiers, the militia, the volunteers, and until they had enough and were ready to quit he could not hope to win. His task, in short, was somewhat similar to that faced by the Americans in Vietnam in the 1960s.

Cornwallis and Clinton sensed this and tried to use Ferguson to rally the Tories, train them, and use them to win the backwoods war. The young Scot was well suited to the task, but he was still too much the conventional professional to properly evaluate his foe. His contempt interfered with his judgment. As a result he was overmatched. Besides that, he had no dream to sell.

While waiting for the crops to ripen, Ferguson moved into the northwestern part of South Carolina. Watching him was Colonel Charles McDowell, commanding the home guard. Much of the militia had gathered, meanwhile, under Rutherford and Caswell for service with Kalb and Gates. Meanwhile, scattered groups of Patriots from occupied Georgia were beating their way northward. Their problem was to get around Ferguson in order to reach McDowell.

Leader of the largest of these bands was Elijah Clarke, a man who would play a curious role in the King's Mountain campaign later that year and who would ultimately attempt to found his own state — Trans-Oconee. Born in 1733, Clarke was a man of little education but possessed of strong leadership qualities. Following him on July 11, 1780, were 140 mounted Georgians. Upon learning that Ferguson was ahead of them, Clarke proposed that his men disband to their homes and wait until the road to the border was clear. Most of the men agreed and so dispersed. John Jones, however, objected. He knew the country well, he said, and could lead a small force to North Carolina despite the Tories. Thirty-five men voted to go with him. Clarke raised no objections, so off they went. Much of the time they posed as Tories marching to join Ferguson. Upon learning of a group of 40 Tories ahead, Jones persuaded a guide to lead them into camp. The surprise was complete. After a quick exchange of shots, some 32 Tories surrendered. All were paroled — a common practice on both sides — and Jones's men, mounted on fresh horses, pushed on to McDowell's camp on the North Pacolet River about twenty miles south of North Carolina. Charles McDowell with three hundred men had arrived there that very day, but everyone was tired and McDowell contented himself with dispatching his brother, Joseph, to scout for the enemy. No word having come from him to indicate an enemy was near, the Patriots settled down to sleep.

Major McDowell had made a wrong turn and overlooked an old Indian fort some twenty miles to the south. The fort was occupied by a combined British and Tory force. When stragglers from the detachment surprised by Jones reached the fort, the British commander sent Major James Dunlap with seventy dragoons to search for Jones. Unaware that Jones had joined with McDowell, the British arrived unseen outside the Patriot camp. A short, bloody fight followed. The dragoons sabered several men in their sleep before McDowell could organize a defense. Jones, the man whose enterprise had brought on the affair, lived despite eight saber cuts. Major Dunlap, realizing he had assaulted a much larger force than anticipated, quickly retreated into the night. He lost two killed and two wounded while the Patriots counted eight dead and thirty wounded. Not much of a battle, but it explains some things that later puzzled historians. For the Patriot dead included Noah Hampton, son of Colonel Andrew Hampton. According to witnesses, he had been aroused from sleep by a bayonet at his throat and asked his name. "Hampton," he replied. The Tory cursed him for a traitor and killed him.

Colonel Hampton was a native of England who settled in the area south of the present town of Rutherfordton before the Revolution. As a captain of militia, he served against the Highland Scots at Moore's Creek Bridge and won the name of a brave and active patriot. The Tories hated him intensely, and spread that hate among members of his family, as the death of Noah illustrates.

It is perhaps no coincidence that one of nine Tories hung after

King's Mountain was Ambrose Mills — one of the few Tories identified that dark night on the Pacolet. But Colonel Hampton's ire was not directed exclusively against the Tories. He blamed Charles McDowell for failing to take elementary military precautions against a surprise attack. Had more pickets been stationed further from camp, an alarm would have been sounded. McDowell, said Hampton, was inadequate as a field commander.

That judgment was later to be weighed by Sevier, Shelby, Cleveland and Campbell, and found to be valid. Which explains why Major Joseph McDowell commanded Burke County troops at King's Mountain while Colonel Charles McDowell rode alone to Hillsborough with a useless message to Horatio Gates.

But we anticipate. At sunrise McDowell tried to make amends. He dispatched Captain Edward Hampton with fifty mounted men in pursuit of Dunlap. After a ride of two hours they overtook the British force and in a charge worthy of Tarleton they routed the enemy. The pursuit continued to within three hundred yards of Fort Prince, the strong point held by the British. Hampton returned to camp with thirty-five fresh horses and most of the enemy's baggage. Not a man was lost on the adventure and a measure of revenge for Noah Hampton had been secured.

Colonel McDowell ordered his men back toward North Carolina. He had seen enough to realize that help would be needed to stop Ferguson when, inevitably, the British decided to move in force. Couriers were sent over the Blue Ridge to the Watauga County with an urgent appeal to Colonels Sevier and Shelby. In their petition seeking admittance into North Carolina in 1776, both men had pledged that "nothing will be lacking or anything neglected that may add weight to the glorious cause in which we are now struggling." The time had come, said McDowell, to honor that pledge.

Shelby was absent in Kentucky on a land-surveying expedition. Sevier, aware that British agents were urging the Cherokees to rise, did not want to leave. Besides, he was hotly courting

Kate Sherrill and would marry her on August 14. However, Major Charles Robertson was dispatched with a company of riflemen some two hundred strong. Robertson reached McDowell's camp near Cherokee Ford on the Broad River in mid-July. He brought assurance that Shelby would soon join them with additional Watauga troops. Charles McDowell began to feel like a general again.

2

It is necessary at this point to turn to Virginia, where premature action by Tories exposed another phase of Cornwallis's "general Plan."

Governor Thomas Jefferson, a man inclined to take the long view, became worried when Charleston fell. His state had remained largely untouched by war while providing idealism, tobacco, and other supplies to sustain the Cause. His fears seemed realized in July, 1780. An official report to Jefferson from Colonel William Preston of Montgomery County explains why. Dated August 8, it states:

> A most horrid conspiracy amongst the Tories in this county being providentially discovered about 10 days ago, obliged me NOT only to raise militia of the county, but to call for so large a number from the counties of Washington and Botetourt, that there are upwards of 400 men on duty exclusive of a party which I hear Colonel Lynch marched from Bedford toward the Lead Mines yesterday.
>
> Colonel Hugh Crockett sent two young men amongst the Tories as Tory officers, with whom they agreed to embody to a very great number near the Lead Mines the 25th instant, and after securing that place to overrun the County with the assistance of British troops who they were made to believe would

meet them and relieve the CONVENTION PRISON-
ERS. These they were to arm and THEN SUBDUE
THE WHOLE STATE ...

The British troops were supposed to come through the mountains from North Carolina as well as from the Chesapeake Bay
area where they were to be landed from an invasion fleet, the
"lead mines" were located near present day Wytheville and the
"Convention Prisoners" were held near Charlottesville.

The prisoners were remains of the British army surrendered
by General John Burgoyne on October 17, 1777, at Saratoga,
New York. Under the terms of the "convention" by which they
capitulated, they were supposed to have been returned to England on parole. For reasons not entirely honorable, this wasn't
done. Instead, the four thousand plus men, half of them Hessians,
were shuffled about for almost two years before arriving in
Charlottesville. Jefferson, who lived there, became fast friends
with many of the officers. A touch of European culture was
welcome in the foothills of the Blue Ridge. The men settled
down in barracks and planted gardens. They seemed quite
happy, but, of course, represented a very real danger if released
and armed.

The lead mines were essential to the Patriots' war effort. Jefferson, in his "Notes on Virginia," has given this description of
what he considered a valuable natural resource:

> On the Great Kanhaway, opposite to the mouth of
> Cripple creek and about twenty-five miles from our
> southern boundary in the County of Montgomery, are
> mines of lead. The metal is mixed, sometimes with
> earth and sometimes with rock which requires the
> force of gunpowder to open it; and it is accompanied
> with a portion of silver too small to be worth sepa-
> ration under any process hitherto attempted there.
> The proportion yielded is from fifty to eighty pounds
> of pure metal from one hundred pounds of washed

ore . . . They have produced sixty tons of lead in the year; but the general quantity is from twenty to twenty-five tons. The present furnace is a mile from the ore bank and on the opposite side of the river. The ore is first wagoned to the river, a quarter of a mile, then ladened on board of canoes and carried across the river, which is about two hundred yards wide, and then again taken into wagons and carried to the furnace. From the furnace the lead is transported one hundred and thirty miles along a good road leading through the Peaks of Otter to Lynch's ferry, or Winston's on James River, from whence it is carried by water about the same distance to Westham.

The lead from the Virginia mines was badly needed in the South during that "battle summer" of 1780, as some papers found many years later in the home of William Lenoir make plain. Datelined Richmond, June 10, 1780, is a letter directed to Colonel Benj. Cleveland in Wilkes County:

Sir —
I received an express from Genl. Rutherford ordering me to raise fifty Light Horse and march to Creswell Mines for one ton of lead to be carried by the Light Horse to Salisbury. I start tomorrow. The General orders me to send you the same instructions, requiring you to go as soon as possible. I shall be there before you and leave a ton for you. You are to hold every effective man in your Regiment in readiness to march at an hour's notice and have him fixed with a gun and a sling and a spantoon.
These orders for want of an opportunity of sending you an express, he ordered me to forward, which I hereby comply with and am Sir,
Your obedient Servt.

The name has been torn off the paper. On the back of it the ever-ready Cleveland wrote this message to Captain Lenoir:

> Sir —
>
> I have received the within orders. You will proceed to raise 15 men in your company. They must find themselves and you must meet at Capt. Allen's 19th of this instant. Early in the day.
>
> Benj. Cleveland

Below the order, Lenoir listed in his handwriting the names of the men who accompanied him.

It was a timely expedition. The men from the eastern slope of the Blue Ridge arrived in the middle of a civil war and found themselves shooting lead as well as transporting it. Cleveland worked closely with Colonel William Campbell of Washington County, Virginia, and together they broke up the concentration of Tories and hunted them up and down the New River. Several hangings were joint affairs, such as the one at Peach Bottom when Zachariah Goss, one of Plundering Sam Brown's gang, was strung up while Cleveland and Campbell watched.

The Campbell clan emigrated to Ireland from Scotland about 1600, and came to Virginia in 1730. William was born in 1745, an only son. He was given the best education available, and at age twenty-two moved to the Holston River area to settle on land his father had acquired. Eager for action, he joined Colonel Christian's regiment during Lord Dunmore's War. Unhappily, Christian did not reach Point Pleasant until the day after that bitter battle was fought, and Campbell came home with sword still sheathed. But not for long. Appropriately, he served under General Andrew Lewis, the grim-faced commander at Point Pleasant, in driving Lord Dunmore off Gwynn Island, the last bit of Virginia real estate the royal governor controlled. That battle on July 9, 1766, ended when Campbell's men appeared. Shouting "The shirt-men are coming," the British troops fled to their ships. Examination proved, however, that smallpox killed more British troops than did the Patriots.

Shortly after the battle, Campbell won a major victory on another field — the hand of Elizabeth Henry, sister of Patrick Henry. Their life was hectic. One Sunday when returning from church with his wife and friends, he noticed a man on horseback approaching. The man abruptly turned off into the woods. A member of the party recognized him as Francis Hopkins, infamous Tory counterfeiter and fugitive. Campbell immediately gave chase. When Hopkins tried to ford the Holston, Campbell followed him into the water and there a desperate struggle took place. Campbell, a huge man of enormous strength, took a knife from the Tory and dragged him ashore. There, with help from his friends, he administered justice. Then Campbell rode back to his wife, who asked:

"What did you do with him, Mr. Campbell?"

"Oh, we hung him, Betty," replied Campbell.

And the couple rode on home from church.

It can be seen then, that Campbell and Cleveland had a lot in common: physical size, patriotic zeal, and a belief that the best Tory was a dead Tory. Yet it would be unfair to assume that either man enjoyed doing what he considered to be his duty. There was a time back on the Yadkin when a youth of thirteen implored Cleveland not to hang a notorious villain just captured. The man had been wounded in the fight and, altogether, was rather a pathetic figure.

"Jimmie, my son," said Cleveland gently, "he is a bad man; we must hang all such dangerous Tories and get them out of their misery."

And with tears coursing down his cheeks, he did just that. The tears, of course, were for the boy.

But Cleveland and Campbell were not the only men busy with a rope in southern Virginia that summer of 1780. The same Colonel Charles Lynch mentioned by Preston won such a reputation in Bedford County as a hangman, that his name became

synonymous with summary justice. Or injustice. Such words
and phrases as "lynch," a "lynching," "lynch law," and "Judge
Lynch," go back to that desperate summer when civil war was
ruthlessly ended. Of course the city of Lynchburg, Virginia, can
also be traced to the Lynch family of that period, and several
attempts to change the name have been defeated.

Even such a staunch supporter of due process and the rights
of man, Governor Jefferson, condoned what was done. In an official letter dated August 1, 1780, Jefferson told Colonel Lynch:

> It gives me real concern to find that there is any
> one citizen in the commonwealth so insensible of the
> advantages of which himself and his posterity must
> derive from the present form of government as com-
> pared to what they can expect on return to dominion
> under a foreign state as to wish to return to it. I sup-
> pose they have materially considered the matter before
> they took the dangerous step they ventured on, and
> that they have made up their minds and reasoning on
> the subject is vain. It remains to determine what shall
> be done. The most rigorous decisive measures should
> be continued for seizing everyone on whom probable
> proof of guilt shall appear . . .
>
> Your activity on this occasion deserves commenda-
> tion and meets it from the Executive. The method of
> seizing them at once, which you have adopted, is
> much the best. No expense of guard must be spared
> as far as they shall be found necessary, and the sooner
> those found guilty can be sent down the better. The
> attorney for the Commonwealth in your county will
> doubtless advise you on your proceedings to which I
> can add nothing but an exhortation but to continue
> the energy with which you have begun to suppress
> these parricides of their country before they shall have
> further leisure to draw other innocent men into the
> same danger.

No doubt Lynch exceeded his instructions, but men understood each other in those days and it is quite possible he had a perfect understanding of what was wanted. To make certain he would suffer no legal reaction, the Virginia legislature passed special acts making legal all executions conducted by the various militia officers during the Tory uprising. That got Campbell off the hook as well as Lynch.

When the danger was past, Campbell helped Cleveland deliver the needed lead to Salisbury as ordered. He spent several weeks in the Yadkin area, and even chased down a few Tories. The pro-British Moravians reported that he and his men were much nicer to them than were the Wilkes County militia under Captain Lenoir.

When Campbell got home in September, he received an urgent message from Isaac Shelby. The enemy now was Patrick Ferguson, and he was threatening to cross the mountains and lay waste the country. Shelby thought something should be done about it.

3

Isaac Shelby, son of a distinguished Indian fighter, was born in Maryland in 1750, won military glory in the Carolinas, and was elected to high office in Kentucky.

Of Welsh descent, Shelby received such education as was possible on his father's plantation — a good one by the standards of the day if his writings are any indication. He became a surveyor and a deputy sheriff as well.

In 1771, the family moved to the Holston River area in what was then believed to be Virginia but later proved to be North Carolina. Today, of course, it is Tennessee. Cattle raising was the principal occupation. An early visitor, as has been related, was John Sevier. The two men visited James Robertson's settlement on the Watauga, and lasting friendships were established.

Shelby was a man of great physical strength, tall and well muscled, with a hawklike profile and a complexion that grew florid with age. Dignified in appearance, he possessed the ability to gain the confidence of other men. Perhaps the training he received from his father, Evan, accounts in part for it. In 1774, when the son was given a commission as a lieutenant in the militia by Colonel William Preston, the father was unsatisfied with his son's demeanor. It lacked respect, he felt. As Isaac took his seat, Evan growled:

"Get up, you dog you, and make your obeisance to the Colonel."

And Isaac did.

The purpose of the commission was to permit Isaac to serve as his father's aide in the campaign against the Shawnees that ended with the battle of Point Pleasant. Isaac's account of that battle has been much utilized by such historians as Theodore Roosevelt.

"So completely were the Savages chastised that they could not be induced by British Agents among them, neither to the North nor to the South, to commence hostilities against the United States before July 1776," said Shelby in his unpublished autobiography.

Following the battle, a fort was built on the site overlooking the Ohio and Shelby was made second in command. He remained in that post until 1775 when, following the meeting at Sycamore Shoals with the Cherokees, he went to Kentucky to survey the lands purchased by Judge Henderson. After twelve months "in the cane brakes" his health broke down. Shelby blamed "continued exposure to wet and cold and living without bread or salt." He went home to find an appointment waiting as "captain of a minute company by the Committee of Safety of Virginia."

Before the signing of the Treaty of Long Island of the Holston with the Cherokees in 1777, large numbers of troops — including those commanded by Cleveland and Lenoir — were stationed on the western slopes. Shelby was given the task of supplying rations. As he put it: "These supplies could not possibly be obtained nearer than Staunton in Virginia, a distance of near three hundred miles." So well did he perform this difficult assignment that he was given others of a similar nature over the next three years. He worked for Virginia until early in 1780 when a survey proved that his Holston property was inside North Carolina. The new county of Sullivan was created and Shelby was commissioned colonel of the militia.

As soon as the snow melted that spring, Shelby went to Kentucky to relocate and secure those lands he had marked out for himself in 1775. He was there in bluegrass country when word of the fall of Charleston crossed the mountains. Immediately he returned home, "determined," as he put it in his unpublished autobiography, "to enter the service of his country until her independence was secured for he could not remain a cool spectator of a contest in which his dearest interests were at stake."*

Waiting for him was the opportunity he sought: an appeal from Colonel Charles McDowell of Burke County to bring troops to stop the enemy even then approaching the frontier from the south. Major Robertson had already marched from adjoining Washington County with all the troops Sevier could spare. Shelby mustered the militia in Sullivan and called for volunteers for the standard sixty-day tour of duty asked of men who would soon have crops to harvest. With almost two hundred mounted riflemen he crossed the mountains. The journey was just as long, just as difficult as the later expedition to King's Mountain, but it has received little attention from historians, who have preferred to regard the second jaunt as an isolated, unique incident.

It was July 25th when Shelby's men joined McDowell at the Cherokee Ford of the Broad River some five miles inside South Carolina at just about the place where Interstate 85 crosses the Broad today. Within hours, the ubiquitous Elijah Clarke showed up as well, with a small band of Georgians and a plan to attack

---

* Shelby's autobiography was written in the third person.

a Tory force making its headquarters in an old Indian outpost known as Fort Thickety. The Tories were commanded by Captain Patrick Moore, brother of John Moore who had led the Tories to defeat at Ramseur's Mill. From Fort Thickety, his men sallied forth to raid and rob Patriots throughout the area. Clarke thought it a worthy idea to stifle Moore.

Charles McDowell was in his glory. Now he could play general to his heart's content, remaining with most of his men in a strong central position while sending out such enterprising individuals as Clarke and Shelby to hit and run. After all, Cornwallis was employing Ferguson and Tarleton in the same fashion, wasn't he? So consent for an attack on Thickety Fort was given and away went Clarke and Shelby with five hundred mounted men. Major Robertson was along and with him was Valentine Sevier, brother of John Sevier, which perhaps explains why some writers have insisted that Shelby's old friend was involved. War had its charms for John Sevier, but, as noted, so did Bonnie Kate. Just two weeks after the battle of Thickety Fort, he married Kate — his first wife having died early in the year after a long illness.

Details of the fort's defenses were included in a scrap of letter found among Ferguson's personal effects at King's Mountain:

> It had an upper line of loopholes and was surrounded by a strong abatis, with only a small wicket to enter by. It had been put in thorough repair at the request of the garrison, which consisted of neighboring militia that had come to the fort; and was defended by eighty men against two or three hundred banditti without cannon, and each man was of opinion that it was impossible to take ...

The Patriots left camp at sunset, rode twenty miles through the night, and arrived outside the fort at sunrise. A demand for surrender was refused. Shelby's men then surrounded the fort and approached within two hundred yards. Preparations for storming the fort were made.

Captain Moore, watching these preparations, must have remembered his brother's adventures. When a second demand for surrender was made, he suddenly agreed to do so on condition the garrison be put on parole not to serve again unless exchanged. According to Shelby, ninety-two Loyalists and one British officer — "left there to discipline them" — were captured along with 250 stands of arms "well charged with ball and buckshot and well disposed at the different portholes."

That fragmented British account found on another stricken field was quite bitter:

> The officer next in command, and all the others, gave their opinion for defending it, and agree in their account that Patrick Moore, after proposing a surrender, acquiesced in their opinion and offered to go and signify as much to the rebels, but returned with some Rebel officers whom he put in possession of the gate and place, who were instantly followed by their men and the fort was full of Rebels to the surprise of the garrison. He pleaded cowardice, I understand.

Ferguson, made thus rudely aware of Shelby and Clarke's presence in the area, made several attempts to trap them. He almost succeeded on August 7. The little army stopped for the night on Fair Forest Creek, west of Cedar Springs. Scouts were sent out. The night passed without incident, but next morning at daybreak a shot was heard and the scouts came rushing in to report the British were within a half mile. The shot, it was decided later, was fired by a friendly Tory who claimed it was an accident. Hastily, the men retreated toward Cedar Springs until they found suitable ground and there they formed their line. The British force was led by Major Dunlap and consisted of dragoons and mounted infantry. In the hand-to-hand combat that followed, Clarke was wounded and then captured. As two husky Tories were leading him away, he broke loose and knocked one of the men down. The other ran. Clarke, blood streaming from his neck, rejoined the battle.

The long rifles of the mountaineers had taken a deadly toll before the dragoons closed, however, and Dunlap was beaten back. An hour or two after pursuit ended, Ferguson with his main army came up. Shelby ordered a retreat, but it was a fighting retreat with the Americans "forming frequently on advantageous ground." Finally Ferguson's men, weary from a long march, gave up and the Patriots escaped with some twenty prisoners.

The next target chosen by Colonel McDowell for his energetic allies was a detachment of some two hundred Tories stationed at Musgrove Mill on the Enoree River, a tributary of the Broad. The spot was much deeper in South Carolina than McDowell had hitherto ventured, and was within striking distance of the British fort known as Ninety-Six — so named because it was erroneously believed to be ninety-six miles from Fort Prince George in Cherokee country. Major Joseph McDowell went along, as did Captains David Vance and Valentine Sevier. Also in the expedition was Colonel James Williams of South Carolina, who had joined McDowell with a handful of men a few days before.

Ferguson's main army lay across the direct route to Musgrove Mill, so the Patriots cut through the woods to get around him, and then with darkness to hide them rode briskly down a good road. "They rode very hard all night," Shelby noted, "the greatest part of the way in a traveling gait, and just at dawn of day, about half a mile from the Enemies camp, met a strong patrol party. A short skirmish ensued and several of them were killed."

Realizing the chance to surprise the enemy was lost, the attackers halted on top of a ridge to take counsel. At that point a pro-British farmer wandered in and informed Shelby with no little satisfaction that the British had been reinforced the evening before by some six hundred men. Colonel Alexander Innes was there along with Captain Abraham dePeyster. The realization that instead of unsteady Tories, they were now facing a much larger group of trained provincials led by British officers, gave Shelby and his men much to think about. They had trapped themselves, it seemed, slipping into a vise. This formidable force was in front and Ferguson was in the rear.

What to do? As Shelby put it:

> To march on and attack the enemy seemed improper. To attempt an escape from the enemy in the rear appeared improbably, broke down as were most of the Americans and their horses . . . They instantly determined to form a breastwork of old logs and brush near the spot and make the best defence in their power, for by this time the drums and bugle horns of the Enemy were distinctly heard in their camp on the high ground across the River.

The Patriots then devised a trap of their own. Captain Shadrach Inman, one of Clarke's men, was sent forward with twenty-five horsemen to fake an attack on the British camp. As soon as the enemy responded, he was to retreat as if in disorder across the ford, drawing the British after him in the belief the entire attacking force had been routed. Shelby credits Inman with the idea.

It worked — beautifully.

The mountaineers and their allies waited — Shelby in command of the right, Clarke the center, and Williams the left. A reserve of forty men was placed in the center. Orders were passed along the line not to shoot "until you can see the buttons on their coat" and not then unless a specific command to fire was issued. That order came when the enemy was seventy yards away, and the fire was "most destructive."

The Loyalists recoiled, but such was the pressure of their numbers behind them, they soon came on again. From their breastworks, from trees and fences, the mountaineers poured in their fire. Even so, Shelby was at last pushed back at bayonet point by overwhelming numbers. Clarke sent the reserve to his aid and William Smith, one of the Watauga men, shot Colonel Innes from his horse. The rest of the Backwater Men raised an

Indian war whoop and charged forward. The British, disheartened by the fall of their leaders — practically all the Tory officers in the battle were killed or wounded by the sharpshooters — began to retreat.

Still whooping, the Patriots followed. Captain Inman, the hero of the day, was killed as he led the pursuit and was buried on the spot. The retreat became a rout as, panic-stricken, the British and Tories splashed into the river and began wading across. An attempt to make a stand on the far bank ended when a detachment of mountaineers under Captain Sam Moore crossed up river and took the fugitives in the rear. After that it was every man for himself on the long run to Ninety-Six.

The British lost sixty-three killed, about ninety wounded, and seventy captured. The Patriots reported four killed and nine wounded. Bullet marks on the trees, examined after the battle, indicated that the British *overshot* their targets while the Patriots' aim was accurate. In more ways than one, the Battle of Musgrove Mill was a prelude to King's Mountain.

Glorious as was the victory, the opportunity for a greater one seemed to exist. According to Shelby, the victors "returned to their horses and mounted with a determination to be in Ninety-Six before night, it being less than thirty miles distant." Other reports indicate that the garrison at Ninety-Six was ready to panic as word came in that a force of 5,000 Patriots was about to overwhelm it. The exaggeration of the enemy's strength seems to have been a routine reaction to bad news — it was to happen again after King's Mountain.

Just as Shelby and his men were ready to ride, a courier from Colonel McDowell came dashing up on a lathered horse. He brought a letter McDowell had received the night before from General Caswell, informing McDowell "of the defeat of the American grand army under General Gates" two days before at Camden. Caswell advised McDowell "to get out of the way" in the belief that the enemy would cut up all remaining "corps of the American Armies within their reach."

General Caswell was a former governor and Shelby recognized his handwriting. Otherwise he would have suspected a Tory trick. With the Caswell letter, McDowell had included a note advising that he — the cautious commander — would retreat immediately toward Gilbert Town — now the city of Rutherfordton. It can be assumed that this hasty action on the part of McDowell — action which left even his brother in danger — didn't endear the colonel to Shelby. But in the panic after Gates's defeat it was *sauve qui peut*, as America's French allies would say.

The isolated mountaineers changed in an instant from pursuer to pursued, and started north as fast as their weary horses could go. Three men were assigned to each prisoner, taking turns in carrying him double. They passed to the right of Ferguson's camp but, as expected, they were soon being chased. Shelby insists that Abraham dePeyster led the pursuit — dePeyster told him so at King's Mountain — but other authorities suggest it was Frederic dePeyster, the younger brother of Abraham. In any case, the hunt was long and grim. The retreating men ate green corn pulled from its stalk as they rode along, and drank water from the many small streams they passed. The pursuers were at one point only thirty minutes behind their prey, but, luckily for the frontiersmen, they didn't know it. Finally, the British gave up and — faces swollen and half-blind — the victors of Musgrove Mill crossed the line into North Carolina and reached McDowell's new base. Since departing from camp on the night of August 17th, they had traveled over 120 miles with time out only for a battle.

Shelby is not very explicit as to what plans were made when he rejoined McDowell. However, Captain David Vance has left an account which goes into some detail and is confirmed by the best evidence — subsequent events.

According to Vance, Shelby proposed that he and Robertson, with their militia, return to the Western Waters and, in consultation with Colonel Sevier, raise a new army of volunteers. Meanwhile, Colonel Cleveland would be alerted and asked to join the expedition. McDowell would endeavor to save the herds of beef cattle then roaming the mountain valleys from Ferguson, and would keep the westerners informed of Ferguson's movements. Couriers were appointed to pass continually from the Catawba to the Watauga with the latest intelligence. A direct link between Cleveland and Shelby was also arranged — Gideon Lewis and Robert Cleveland were the couriers.

While these plans were being made, Clarke took his men and went back to Georgia, determined to make a surprise attack on Augusta, where a large supply of gifts for the Cherokees had been collected by the British. Colonel Williams took charge of the prisoners and conducted them to Hillsborough, where Gates was trying to rally an army. At Hillsborough he met South Carolina Governor John Rutledge, who promptly made Williams a brigadier general in the mistaken belief he had commanded the troops at Musgrove Mill. Williams, an ambitious man, let him think what he pleased.

Shelby, Robertson, and the rest of the over-the-mountain men went home, their enlistment period having expired. "It was a fact," as Shelby later wrote, "that at that moment there was not the appearance of a corp of Americans embodied anywhere south of Virginia. So great was the panic after Genl. Gates' defeat and Sumter's disaster, that McDowell's whole army broke."

McDowell, ever cautious, waited until September 7, when Ferguson invaded North Carolina and advanced to Gilbert Town. Then he followed Shelby across the mountains and made camp at Sycamore Shoals. Approximately two hundred men were with him. Such a long retreat was hardly necessary, but it is to be assumed that McDowell reasoned he could better stir Shelby and Sevier to action by being on the scene. Certainly, the tales his men told of Tory outrages helped stimulate the recruitment of volunteers.

More help came from Ferguson, who made the mistake of adding insult to injury. He paroled Sam Phillips, a cousin of Shelby who had been captured during the summer, with orders to take a message across the mountains. Phillips obeyed. The message, he said, was that "if the officers west of the mountains did not lay down their opposition to the British arms, he, Ferguson, would march his army over and lay waste their country."

Nothing could have been better calculated to bring the mountaineers running to camp with their long rifles. Such a threat *demanded* a reply. Above the blue hills, the thunderhead grew blacker still.

4

We'll Gather at the River

On September 1, 1780, Lieutenant Anthony Allaire noted in his diary that "Maj. Ferguson joined up again from Camden with the disagreeable news that we were to be separated from the army, and act on the frontiers with the militia."

On September 7 he reported:

"Got in motion at seven o'clock in the morning; crossed Buck creek, and the division line of South and North Carolina; marched six miles farther and halted. Maj. Ferguson, with about fifty of the American Volunteers and three hundred militia, got in motion at six o'clock in the evening and marched to Gilbert Town [Rutherfordton] in order to surprise a party of Rebels that we heard were there."

And so the long-planned invasion of North Carolina was under way.

Lord Cornwallis moved more slowly. It was September 8 before the main army marched out of Camden and up the Great Wagon Road toward Charlotte in the center of the southern boundary. But this wasn't all by any means. Cornwallis's master plan called for troops from Charleston, where Colonel Nisbet

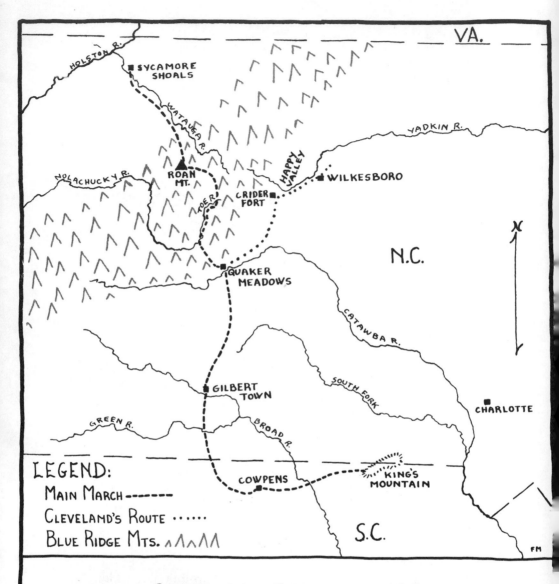

VA.

HOLSTON R.

■ SYCAMORE SHOALS

WATAUGA R.

YADKIN R.

ROAN MT.

TOE R.

CRIDER FORT

HAPPY VALLEY

■ WILKESBORO

NOLACHUCKY R.

N.C.

N

QUAKER MEADOWS

CATAWBA R.

GILBERT TOWN

SOUTH FORK

CHARLOTTE

GREEN R.

BROAD R.

LEGEND:
Main March -------
Cleveland's Route ......
Blue Ridge Mts. ʌʌʌʌʌ

COWPENS

KING'S MOUNTAIN

S.C.

FM

SEPT. 26 – OCT. 7, 1780
LINE OF MARCH – BACKWATER MEN

Balfour commanded, to push northward along the coast and take Wilmington at the mouth of the Cape Fear River. This would give Cornwallis a shorter supply line to the sea, and it would run through the friendly Cross Creek area inhabited by Highland Scots. In addition, a diversionary force under Major General Alexander Leslie was to sail from New York and land in the Chesapeake Bay area of Virginia, where it would move inland to cut off any possible reinforcements to North Carolina from Washington. Originally, of course, there were to be Tory uprisings in North Carolina and Virginia. These had been nipped in the bud, but British agents were making a deal with Dragging Canoe and there was expectation the Cherokees would spread terror around the rim of the Blue Ridge and thus keep the Backwater Men pinned down at home.

While in numbers the British troops probably did not exceed eight thousand, including Tories, the plan was Napoleonic in sweep. Cornwallis had every right to feel proud of it. Nothing similar had been attempted in five years of warfare in America. The Carolina Squeeze would make possible the Chesapeake Squeeze, Cornwallis believed, and that would end the war.

Success seemed but a matter of time to Ferguson as he roamed the foothills of the Blue Ridge. In the absence of organized opposition, many "realists" accepted his thesis that the war was all but over and sought "protection," as it was called, by taking an oath of allegiance. But Ferguson was at least as interested in beeves as in Tories, and in this respect he was sorely disappointed.

Before retiring to Watauga, Shelby had discussed with McDowell plans to drive the vast herds of beef cattle grazing the Catawba meadows back into the hills. McDowell persuaded several ranchers to "take protection" and thus safeguard their herds. Others, who considered such a tactic dishonorable, drove their cattle into the coves of Black Mountain and the Globe — that very area Bishop Spangenberg considered so wild as to have been unvisited by man since the creation. Ferguson, annoyed at finding so few "Whig" beeves available, took counsel with John Carson, one of his new allies of convenience. Carson told him where to look, and Ferguson's men returned with beef from a hundred steers. Only then did they discover they had been outwitted — the beeves belonged to loyal Tories who, however, weren't very loyal after they learned what had happened.

If Ferguson could not tell a Tory bull from a Whig one, he could recognize the symptoms of smallpox and act decisively. One of his officers became ill with the dread disease. On Ferguson's orders he was made comfortable in an isolated cabin, and left there to die. No one dared approach to offer aid, and the cabin remained a plague spot for years until at last someone ventured in to steal the sword and pistol of the long dead soldier. Not even his name survived since, logically, Ferguson was not anxious to report the incident, and the local people had no way of knowing the identity of the unfortunate man.

Major James Dunlap had better luck. He was wounded in a skirmish with McDowell's retreating force near Brindletown and placed with some friendly Tories to recuperate. Word leaked out, however, that he had boasted of killing Noah Hampton in that surprise attack on the Pacolet. Inevitably, a party of pro-Hampton men paid the disabled man a visit. One of them had an additional score to settle — Dunlap had allegedly abducted his fiancee when she refused his advances, and the girl had died. Dunlap was shot as he lay in bed and left for dead. His friends let everyone assume he had died. The location of his supposed grave was pointed out for years and the blood-stained floor planks of his bedroom were preserved long after the house was torn down. The major got away, however, and lived to fight and be captured the following year. This time he was killed — murdered, according to General Andrew Pickens, who offered a reward for his killers.

But not all incidents were tragic. Ferguson, in quest of cattle, penetrated into the mountains to Cathey's Fort on the upper reaches of the Catawba. Hearing that a noted Rebel, Captain Thomas Lytle, lived nearby, Ferguson decided to drop in. Mrs.

Lytle, who was alone at the time, learned that guests were coming and decided to dress up. She would show the handsome British officer that American women could look like ladies even on the frontier. Luckily, her husband had just bought her a new gown and a stylish beaver hat which she had lacked opportunity to wear.

Up came Ferguson at the head of a little troop. Mrs. Lytle came out on the porch in her finery and the officer bowed from his saddle. She dropped a curtsy in reply, and invited him to dismount and partake of refreshment. Politely, he declined. He wanted to see her husband. Alas, her husband wasn't home.

"Madame," said Ferguson, "do you know where he is?"

"To be candid," replied the lady, "I really do not. I only know that he is out with others of his friends whom you call Rebels."

"Well, madame," said the officer, "I have discharged my duty. If he persists in rebellion and comes to harm, his blood be upon his own head."

Mrs. Lytle forgot her concern for appearance and sought to defend her husband's honor.

"I don't know how this war will end," she said, "but I do know my husband will never prove a traitor to his country."

Ferguson smiled. "Mrs. Lytle," he replied, "I admire you as the handsomest woman I have seen in North Carolina, but take my word for it — the rebellion has had its day and is now virtually put down. Give my kind regards to Captain Lytle and tell him to come in. He will not be asked to compromise his honor."

With that the slender young man on the big white horse bowed, and rode away. The exchange had been very civilized. Unfortunately, a straggler spoiled the scene by riding over to Mrs. Lytle and grabbing her beaver hat from her head. He rode off laughing.

The widow Bowman, on the other hand, had the last laugh when a party of Ferguson's men called on her. She was between husbands, her first having been killed at Ramseur's Mill earlier in the year. When she discovered a British officer taking her horse from the stable, she protested. The officer replied most politely:

"Madame, the King hath need of your horse."

Grace Bowman, a woman of decision, stepped inside the house and grabbed her late husband's loaded rifle. Promptly she returned to the yard and pointed it at the officer. "Put that horse back in the stable," she commanded.

"Madame," said the officer, "the King hath no further need of your horse."

Lieutenant Allaire's diary reflects the marching and counter-marching with which Ferguson occupied his men in September. On a Thursday he could report:

"The poor deluded people of this Province begin to be sensible of their error, and come in very fast." The next day Allaire marched to Pleasant Gardens, home of one of the McDowells, and commented: "This settlement is composed of the most violent Rebels I ever saw, particularly the young ladies."

Yet it wasn't bad duty that September in the foothills. Allaire could note that Cane Creek was "so amazingly crooked" it was necessary to cross it "nineteen times in marching four miles." On another day he counted eight wild turkeys while marching along. Gilbert Town, he reported, on marching back to it September 23, "contains one dwelling house, one barn, a blacksmith shop and some outhouses."

On the very next day, Allaire continued, "Five hundred subjects came in, also a number of ladies." Some of the new recruits, Ferguson thanked and sent home. They were no longer needed, he said, since the rebellion in North Carolina was so completely crushed. The disposition of the "ladies" is unclear. Indeed, one may wonder if they were truly ladies in the polite meaning of the word. Certainly, two women attached themselves personally to Ferguson at this time. They are known to history as Virginia Sal, a buxom redhead, and Virginia Paul. Little else is known about them since gentlemen of that day, and historians of the Victorian era that followed, were reluctant to pry into Ferguson's private affairs. It seems safe to assume, however, that the two women provided a variety of services for Ferguson — including the washing of his linen.

But the soft life was about over. His assigned task seemingly completed, Ferguson waited for Cornwallis's next move. His lordship sat at Charlotte, which he had taken after an embarrassingly sharp fight with a handful of Patriots, waiting for his supply trains to come up and for Leslie to land to the north in Virginia. A few bands of guerrillas under Colonel James Davie and Colonel Jethro Sumner buzzed about his ears like hornets and made communications with Ferguson somewhat haphazard, but they offered no serious opposition. More serious was the illness of Tarleton — the cocky cavalry leader had a bad case of the fever as did many of his men. The cavalry was badly misused in his absence but Tarleton took his time about recovering. It was the wrong time to take it.

On September 24, just as Ferguson was preparing to march eastward, a courier arrived from Colonel Thomas Brown at Augusta, Georgia. Ferguson knew Brown as an angry young man who had been tarred and feathered and ridden out of Augusta on a rail at the start of the war. He had raised a body of troops known as the East Florida Rangers and led a series of raids in Georgia. Early in 1780 he returned home, ran out all the Rebels, and settled down in control of the town. One of the men he hated was Elijah Clarke, and Clarke returned the compliment with interest. After leaving Shelby and McDowell, following the Musgrove Mill action, Clarke had gone back to Georgia, raised a new regiment and, in conjunction with Lieutenant Colonel James McCall, assaulted Augusta. The British insisted the whole business was but a raid to steal the gifts given annually to the Cherokees, and they may have been right. Still, those gifts were of unusual importance at a time when Dragging Canoe was on the verge of renewing his vendetta against the white intruder, and their capture might have caused problems for the British agents. As it turned out, a band of Cherokees appeared on the scene and reinforced Brown, who needed all the help he could get. Clarke cut off the water supply to the principal fort, but Brown ordered a well dug and was lucky enough to strike water. Reinforcements finally arrived from Ninety-Six, and Clarke was forced to withdraw his three hundred men. But he was also saddled with four hundred women and children from around Augusta. With their men away and the Indians smelling blood, he didn't dare leave them behind. The vindictive Brown, aware that Clarke would have to travel slowly, proposed to Ferguson that Clarke's line of retreat be intercepted and the troublemaker eliminated once and for all time.

Ferguson thought it an excellent suggestion. He postponed his planned march east to Cornwallis, and sent out scouts to learn the whereabouts of Clarke and his band of pilgrims. That they were headed for the mountains seemed certain, but there were several possible routes. For two days Ferguson waited at Gilbert Town for news. Then he moved three miles and camped again. A day or two later, on September 28, he marched a few more miles, crossing the Broad River. The troops "lay on our arms until four o'clock next morning," as Allaire put it, in expectation of Clarke's coming. Nothing happened. There was little movement for two more days, but on September 30 some news arrived.

It didn't concern Clarke, however. A new menace was afoot.

Next day Ferguson issued a proclamation and couriers rode hard to post it at every crossroad and country store for miles around. Dated from Denard's Ford, Broad River, Tryon County, October 1, 1780, it was addressed "To the Inhabitants of North Carolina." It began:

> Gentlemen:
> Unless you wish to be eat up by an inundation of barbarians, who have begun by murdering an unarmed son before the aged father, and afterwards lopped off his arms, and who by their shocking cruelties and irregularities, give the best proof of their cowardice and

want of discipline; I say, if you wish to be pinioned, robbed, and murdered, and see your wives and daughters, in four days, abused by the dregs of mankind — in short, if you wish or deserve to live and bear the name of men, grasp your arms in a moment and run to camp.

The Backwater men have crossed the mountains; McDowell, Hampton, Shelby and Cleveland are at their head, so that you know what you have to depend upon. If you choose to be pissed upon forever and ever by a set of mongrels, say so at once and let your women turn their backs upon you, and look out for real men to protect them.

Pat Ferguson, Major 71st Regiment

2

It is interesting that of the four leaders named by Ferguson only Shelby was truly a "backwater" man. Hampton, McDowell and Cleveland were men of the eastern waters and, as such, well known and hated by North Carolina Tories. Sevier had not yet fought east of the mountains and Campbell had made only one minor expedition in conjunction with Cleveland. Ferguson, it can be assumed, had never heard of them before. In any case, his purpose in writing the broadside was to arouse the Tories he had permitted to go home, and to do that he needed names they could identify. Shelby's services at Fort Thickety and Musgrove Mill had made him as well-known as McDowell and Cleveland, so he was included along with Hampton, who had a local reputation.

In reporting the murder and mutilation of "an unarmed son before the aged father," Ferguson was trying to inflame opinion by an outright lie. In using the word "piss," however, he was not guilty of vulgarity. For another ten years, until 1790, the London *Times* would use the word without apology. It is rather ironic that various historians such as Draper have substituted such words as "degraded" and "stepped upon" for Ferguson's language, which was perfectly proper for its day. Moreover, they made the change without signifying they had done so, an omission which creates considerable confusion in the mind of the student who lacks access to an uncensored version. More important, the change, and the mock modesty that inspired it, prevented those Victorian gentlemen from explaining certain events that occurred a few days later.

If the language was proper, the reasoning behind the proclamation was as faulty as the message Ferguson sent earlier to Shelby. Far from being inspired to grasp their arms and run to camp, the Tories' reaction was to hold back and await developments. It was one thing to rally to the King when all opposition to him appeared vanquished, but it was something else to do so on the eve of a battle with a horde of mountain men. The Tories may have agreed that their enemies were "mongrels" and "barbarians," but they also knew them to be good fighters. Lacking Ferguson's pride as an officer and a gentleman, they were able to face up to realities in a manner he continued unwilling to do.

Shelby, of course, needed no threat to arouse him to action. He had made up his mind to fight back in May when word of Charleston's fall reached him in Kentucky. Neither did Sevier need a spur, although it may be assumed he was not anxious to leave his bride. Yet he was no callow youth, and Shelby did not hesitate upon receiving Ferguson's message to ride fifty miles to Jonesboro, where Sevier was attending a horse race.

In conference, the two men agreed the threat from Ferguson would be useful. Not every mountaineer was concerned with the principles of collective freedom — not enough, at least, to go traipsing over the hills to fight strangers — but no hillbilly liked to be threatened either. The men of Watauga had long before learned the value of preventive war in conflicts with the Indians. If there was even a chance that Ferguson might come calling, well, the sensible thing was to go after him first.

As Shelby wrote:

"After some consultation we determined to march with all the men we could raise, and to attempt to surprise Ferguson by attacking him in his camp, or, at any rate, before he was prepared for us. We accordingly appointed a time and place of rendezvous."

The time was September 25; the place was Sycamore Shoals on the Watauga.

Some money was necessary. While the men would be volunteers, serving without pay and supplying their rifles and hunting knives, they would need powder, shot, and food. Their horses would need corn and shoes.

To get the funds Sevier went to John Adair, entry-taker for Sullivan County. A native of Antrim County, Ireland, Adair brought his family to America in 1772, and moved from Maryland to the Holston River area a year later. In Adair's keeping was the sum of $12,735, which he had collected from land sales but because of the crisis across the mountains had been unable to deliver to the state's treasury. Sevier asked for the money, assuring Adair that he and Shelby would see that it was repaid. The new American didn't hesitate:

"Colonel Sevier," he is reported to have said, "I have no right to make any such disposition of this money; it belongs to North Carolina. But if the country is overrun by the British, liberty is gone — so let the money go too. Take it."

Having turned over the cash, Adair and his son promptly signed up too, and are among those listed as having fought at King's Mountain. In 1832, John Adair, Jr., then seventy-eight years old, filed an application for a pension in Wayne County, Kentucky, for his Revolutionary War services. All he could remember of the King's Mountain campaign was that he served under a man named Campbell.

Getting Campbell back into action was no easy task. Following the two-day conference with Sevier, Shelby "hurried home" and "wrote to Col. Campbell and sent my brother, Moses Shelby, with it to his house, a distance of forty miles."

Campbell, as noted earlier, had just returned home from his

campaign against the Tories — a campaign which had carried him across the mountains and down the Yadkin to the Moravian towns founded by Bishop Spangenberg. He was familiar with Cornwallis's plan to invade Virginia and he assumed the invasion would follow the Great Wagon Road from Charlotte to Salisbury and into the heart of the Old Dominion. He told Moses Shelby to wait while he drafted a reply. Sorry, he said, in effect, but he was going to march his men out of the mountains eastward by way of Flower Gap and would await Cornwallis's coming on the border.

"I was much disappointed," said Shelby. "I was unwilling that the whole force should be drawn from Sullivan and Washington Counties and leave them exposed to the Cherokees from whom we were daily threatened with a heavy attack."

So Shelby wrote another letter giving "additional reasons for him to join with us." That the letter stressed the possibility that a successful strike at Ferguson might cause Cornwallis to delay or drop the invasion of Virginia is almost certain. Moses Shelby carried the letter again, and this time he brought back agreement:

"Campbell replied that he would join with his whole force and that he would come by my house and go with me to the rendezvous (He did so for he came to my residence on Saturday evening the 23rd, and we started from there on Sunday morning the 24th) while his men marched down a nearer way by what was then called the Watauga Road."

A second letter was sent to Colonel Arthur Campbell, brother-in-law of William Campbell and county lieutenant of Washington County, Virginia. In this letter, Shelby described the woes of Colonel McDowell and his men, who had been driven from their homes by the ruthless Ferguson. Arthur Campbell was touched. Much later he was to write:

"The tale of McDowell's men was a doleful one, and tended to excite the resentment of the people who, of late, had become inured to danger by fighting the Indians, and who had an utter detestation of the tyranny of the British Government."

So resentful did the Virginians become, that after William Campbell had departed with two hundred men for Sycamore Shoals, another two hundred rallied at the mustering place and demanded a part in the campaign. Arthur Campbell hurriedly led them to the Watauga and turned them over to "Big Bill." Then he went home, wondering how he would defend the frontier if the Cherokees went on a rampage.

The Indian danger was very much on the minds of Shelby and Sevier as well. Fortunately, the year before, James Robertson from his base on the Cumberland had led an expedition against the new Indian towns near Lookout Mountain. Most of the warriors were away in the service of Governor Henry "the Hair Buyer" Hamilton, British commander at Detroit, but Robertson destroyed the towns and the granaries they contained. One granary alone was estimated to hold 20,000 bushels of corn.

Robertson's action bought some time for the Watauga settlers. Working also in their favor was Dragging Canoe's realization that he had acted prematurely in 1776. This time, he decided, he would wait until the British were close at hand before ordering out his braves. Sevier's spies told him of this decision and the information confirmed his opinion that the attack on Ferguson would have to be lightning fast. He arranged for scouts to keep watch on the Cherokees and for couriers to bring him word wherever he might be of an impending assault. With this out of the way, he felt better about leaving his bride behind.

By her marriage, Bonnie Kate had become the stepmother of ten children. Over the years she would give birth to eight of her own, but in 1780 she was trying to accept the responsibility for those on hand. Joseph, the oldest son at eighteen, was to accompany his father. James, who was almost sixteen, thought he was man enough to carry a rifle too. He appealed to his new mother.

"Here, Mr. Sevier," said Mrs. Sevier, "is another of your boys who wants to go with his father and brother to the war — but we have no horse for him, and, poor fellow, it is a great distance to walk."

A horse was found for James, and he rode proudly as a private with his brother. Two of Sevier's brothers also made the trip as captains, Valentine and Robert. Shelby, unmarried, had no sons, but his brothers went along: Major Evan Shelby, Jr., and Captain Moses Shelby.

A relative by marriage of Sevier's first wife was John Crockett, the father of the legendary Davy Crockett. But let Davy tell it:

> My father's name was John Crockett, and he was of Irish descent. He was either born in Ireland or on a passage from that country to America across the Atlantic. He was by profession a farmer, and spent the early part of his life in the state of Pennsylvania. The name of my mother was Rebecca Hawkins. She was an American woman born in the state of Maryland between New York and Baltimore. It is likely I may have heard where they were married, but if so, I have forgotten. It is, however, certain that they were, or else the public would never have been troubled with the history of David Crockett, their son.
>
> I have an imperfect recollection of the part which I have understood my father took in the revolutionary war. I personally know nothing about it, for it happened to be a little before my day; but from himself, and many others who were well acquainted with its troubles and afflictions, I have learned that he was a soldier in the revolutionary war, and took part in that bloody struggle. He fought, according to my information, in the battle at King's Mountain against the British and tories ...

Three other Crocketts were with John at King's Mountain. No less than twelve Campbells from Washington County, Virginia, were in the force — all of them in one way or another related to their commander. But most indicative of all, perhaps, were fifty-nine men whose names began with "Mc." They ranged from McAden to McWaters, and they came impartially from North

Carolina, Virginia, and the future state of Tennessee. Nothing better illustrates the importance of the Scotch-Irish as an ethnic presence in this association of free men.

Sycamore Shoals had seen colorful gatherings in the past — specifically five years earlier when the Cherokee chiefs met to sell Kentucky to Judge Henderson — but none compared to the vast throng that now gathered by the broken waters of the Watauga. Women and children were there to bid their sons, lovers, and husbands, their fathers and brothers, a proud farewell. But more was involved. The crops were in the barn, the gold and crimson were on the leaves, and it was Revival Time. Always in the past had the mountain folk heeded the words of Jeremiah: "The harvest is past, the summer is ended, and we are not saved." Now patriotism mingled with religious fervor to create intense excitement, and it was time to hear from the Reverend Samuel Doak — a preacher for all occasions.

The parents of Sam Doak got married on the boat bringing them from Ireland and settled in Augusta County, Virginia, where in 1749 their son was born. At age sixteen he enrolled in a school taught by Archibald Alexander, a school that eventually moved to another location and became Washington and Lee University. To finance this education, young Doak sold his birthright to his brothers, and went on to attend the College of New Jersey, now Princeton University. After still more study at the College of Hampden-Sidney, he was licensed to preach on October 31, 1777. His sister, Elizabeth Thankful Doak, had married and was living in the Watauga Settlement, so he moved there and bought a farm. He became, however, something of a circuit rider since preachers were in short supply and great demand. In the years following the Revolution he became an educator of note, founding two colleges. Having been given a small library of classical books, he transported it by packhorses some five hundred miles across the mountains. At age sixty-five he began the study of chemistry *and* of Hebrew, and soon was able to teach in both disciplines. A tall man with broad shoulders and a deep

95

chest, he was commanding in appearance and possessed a voice full of thunder and lightning.

The sycamores still thrust upward along the white water of Sycamore Shoals — and three trees grow from the stump of the one under which the Reverend Mr. Doak stood to preach his most historic sermon on September 26, 1780.

Strictly speaking, perhaps, it wasn't a sermon but a prayer. Today's observer might find it difficult to make a distinction. Prayers tended to become rather long-winded and complicated and were directed at the Lord rather than, as in a sermon, at sinful man. The ministers, with all respect, recognized that the Lord was always busy and might overlook some detail unless it was called specifically to His attention and justified.

So Reverend Doak spoke of the good men assembled before him, and of the good women they were leaving behind. He discussed the British and the Tories, pointing out their shameful deeds and sinful ways, and he reminded the Lord that the battle for Liberty was at a critical stage. This suggested another struggle for Liberty — the battle of the Children of Israel against the Midianites, and he refreshed the Lord's memory as to details.

As the mountain men in their hunting shirts stood bareheaded under the warm September sun, their wives and sweethearts at their side, the Reverend Doak lifted his eyes to the blue barrier of the mountains above which the sun had risen, and recounted the saga of Gideon and the Lord.

And he quoted aloud the words of Gideon to his chosen three hundred:

" 'When I blow with a trumpet, I and all that are with me, then blow yet the trumpets also on every side of all the camp and say, "The sword of the Lord, and of Gideon." ' "

Entranced, as if a vision had appeared along the blue peaks to the southeast, the Reverend Doak repeated:

"The sword of the Lord, and of Gideon."

And his people answered, "Amen!"

The preacher held wide his arms and now he spoke to the congregation.

"Let that be your battle cry: the sword of the Lord and of Gideon."

Like slow thunder came the reply: "The sword of the Lord and of Gideon."

And then the men mounted horse and turned up Gap Creek toward the blue mountains. Behind them they left the chatter of water over the rocks and the sobs of women who, in respect, had held back tears until they could do no harm. The "preacher" passed among them, giving words of solace mingled with gentle rebukes for those whose faith seemed unequal to the circumstances.

3

For David Vance the trip over the mountains to Watauga with McDowell's men had been a visit home, but he was anxious to get back to Burke County and see his wife and children.

Vance was of Scotch-Irish descent, the eldest of eight children. His father moved to southwestern Virginia but David, having attained his majority, wandered across the mountains and married Priscilla Brank in Burke County. Like William Lenoir, he combined schoolteaching with land surveying, and, like Lenoir, he grabbed his rifle when war began. Commissioned an ensign in the Second North Carolina Continental Regiment, he was soon promoted to lieutenant. The regiment was sent north to fight under General Washington and it suffered heavily at Brandywine from the fire of Ferguson's crack rifle corps armed with his breechloader. The winter of Valley Forge followed and Vance went cold and hungry with thousands of his companions while the farmers of Pennsylvania sold their produce to the British in Philadelphia for hard cash. From Valley Forge he took a Spanish milled dollar, presented to him by George Washington as a prize for victory in a "running contest."

The North Carolina regiment was so badly decimated by battle and illness, it was consolidated with other regiments. Vance and several officers were sent home to train militia units. In that relatively calm period he was able to resume teaching while living with his family near the present town of Morganton. Colonel McDowell promoted him to captain, and called him to duty early in 1780. He fought with Major Joseph McDowell at Ramseur's Mill and with Shelby and Clarke at Musgrove Mill. When McDowell retreated across the mountains, Vance went along. Now he was returning.

The little army of which Vance was now a part consisted of 1,040 men — if the official report is accurate. Campbell commanded 400, Sevier and Shelby 240 each, and there were 160 refugees from Burke under McDowell and Hampton. No one wore a military uniform — the hunting shirt and trouser made from homespun, with leggings on the legs and a fur-skin cap on the head was the usual dress. Around the waist was a belt from which was hung a knife, a shot bag, a pouch for parched corn, and perhaps a tin cup. From around the neck was suspended the powder horn to fuel the deadly Dickert Rifle.

The rifle has been much abused by historians and deserves a few words of clarification. It has often been referred to as "the Kentucky Rifle" and occasionally as the "Deckhard Rifle," but its name belongs to the man who created it — Jacob Dickert of Lancaster, Pennsylvania. It had a barrel some thirty inches long, and a short stock of from twelve to eighteen inches. Bullets varied from thirty to seventy to the pound of lead. The barrel had a spiral groove and was remarkably accurate at long distances. Some criticized the time required to load it, but mountain men by dint of constant practice had eliminated that as a problem. Indeed, some frontiersmen had learned to load the rifle while on the dead run. Lewis Wetzel, the "Deathwind" of the upper Ohio, once killed three Indians as they chased him through the forest glades. The others abandoned the pursuit at that point.

The line of march was almost due south to the head of Gap Creek, between Greer and Jenkins mountains. Then the men turned eastward around the shoulder of Stone Mountain to Tiger Valley. Crossing between Fork Mountain and Ripshin Ridge, they reached the Doe River. The Doe was a narrow but swift little stream whose source was high on Roan Mountain. They followed it until dark, reaching the "Resting Place" or *Aquone*, as the Cherokees called it, and there they stopped for the night after a march of some twenty miles.

The "Resting Place" was a natural shelter, a large rock jutting out of a hill to form a semi-cave. It is big enough for a party of Indians, perhaps, but hardly large enough to accommodate an army. Today, a bronze plaque is affixed to the rock. The inscription:

FIRST NIGHT ENCAMPMENT
of
King's Mountain Men
Sept. 26, 1780
"They trusted in God
And kept their powder dry."

Generations of young people have added their endorsement with paint brushes.

Next day, Wednesday the 27th, they moved on up Doe River to the very foot of the mountain. The impossibility of driving cattle across the peaks ahead became apparent, so after only four miles a halt was called and the cattle slaughtered. Then, unencumbered, they followed an old hunting trail known as "Bright's Trace" up to Carver's Gap. As the crow flies it was perhaps not much more than eight miles, but at this juncture vertical distance was of more importance than horizontal.

Sycamore Shoals and the broad valley of the Watauga are

about 1,580 feet high. Carver's Gap is 5,512 feet above sea level. Assuming that in reaching the base of the mountain they had climbed 100 feet, this left 3,832 feet for the second day's climb.

At the lower levels they walked under oaks, hickories and maples bright with color, crushing the brittle leaves beneath their feet. But soon the hardwoods gave way to the spruce pine standing straight and tall on the rugged slopes of Roan Mountain. The air got colder and dark clouds hid the mountaintops. Near the top they encountered new-fallen show reaching in depth to their ankles.

The clouds still hung low when they reached the Gap, but before them to the right and left on the shoulders was the "Bald of the Roan." One of the party described it as "a hundred acres of beautiful tableland, in which a spring issued." Today it is dotted with rhododendron bushes whose blooms in late June make the bald a flaming mass of color. On the right towers the Roan High Knob, 6,285 feet high, and on the left is Round Bald Knob, 5,826 feet high.

When the clouds permitted, Vance and his friends could look back to the valley of the Watauga. But most eyes were ahead, studying the blue hills that stretched on and into infinity. This was the high plateau of the Blue Ridge, some forty miles wide at this point, featuring valleys no lower than 3,000 feet above sea level and peaks that reached into the clouds. Near the top of Roan High Knob would be built a century later a resort hotel known as Cloudland. From its wide porches the early bird guest could look *down* on the rising sun as it emerged through the morning mist. From that porch a guest once counted 110 peaks to the south and east, and he didn't count them all. The hotel dining-room straddled the North Carolina–Tennessee line. The 166-room hotel was demolished in 1917, but the view remains.

Dr. Elisha Mitchell, for whom the highest peak east of the Rockies is named, called Roan "the most beautiful of the high mountains — with Carolina at the viewer's feet one side and Tennessee on the other, and a green ocean of mountains rising in tremendous billows around him."

The mountain men were unfazed by the grandeur, unruffled by the cold, but they persisted in calling the whole range on which they stood "the Yellow Mountains." Early histories compounded the error by showing maps which have the western wall labeled as "Smoky Mountains" and the eastern crest as "Yellow Mountains."

On that September day, however, there were matters more pressing than the scenery. A full-dress parade was held on the Bald of the Roan, and it confirmed that the first crisis of the campaign had arrived. Two men from Sevier's company were missing. Sam Chambers was a simple youth, but James Crawford was old enough to know better. No one doubted that Crawford had scented the possibility of a generous reward, and was on his way to Ferguson with news of the expedition. (It was, in fact, the arrival of the two deserters that caused the British officer to issue his "pissing proclamation," as it became known.)

While the men drilled, the colonels took counsel. The possibility that Ferguson, an enterprising officer all agreed, might come to meet his foe, couldn't be discounted. He might even bring some Cherokees along and fashion an ambush. To reduce the risk, it was agreed to change routes. There was some talk of calling the whole thing off since the possibility of surprise had been lost, but the leaders soon agreed that to do so would achieve nothing. For better or worse, the little army would march forward. As if to symbolize that decision, the men were ordered to fire their rifles in salute at the end of the drill. Several men remarked on the thinness of the sound the volley produced — another indication, if one was needed, of the high altitude.

Colonel Charles McDowell and a handful of men were sent on by the shortest route with orders to return as soon as possible with the latest information on Ferguson's movements. The men watched him disappear down the easy path by way of Carter Gap Creek and Roan Valley. Then they turned their horses to the left — eastward — along the side of Round Bald.

Much time had been spent in consultation and parading, so

after only two more miles they camped at a spring near Elk Hollow. At 5,200 feet, the night was cold, but Thursday dawned crisp and clear and the horsemen went down Elk Hollow Branch to Roaring Creek, and followed it to its junction with North Toe River. It was easy going since it was all downhill, a drop of more than a thousand feet. The temperatures climbed as the men descended.

Down the west bank of the carefree Toe they rode, stopping for lunch at a spring where some seventy years later an old sword was found. Which officer lost his weapon and how? History has no answer. South of the village of Plumtree there stands today the Vance Memorial Church — another mark of passage, perhaps.

The river curled and twisted, occasionally doubling back, and its ravines were littered with boulders and fallen trees, but good mileage was achieved. By nightfall the men had come some twenty miles and were at the mouth of Grassy Creek in what today is the beautiful town of Spruce Pine.

At sunrise on Friday, the fourth day of the march, they headed up the valley of Grassy Creek in a southeastern direction, abandoning the Toe. That they were still in the land of the western waters is demonstrated by the Toe, which meandered around until joined by its sister, the South Toe River, and then cut back to the west to become the Nolichucky and emerge from the mountains near Jonesboro — the very place Sevier met with Shelby to plan the expedition.

After marching uphill for some ten miles, the army reached the eastern crest of the Blue Ridge and stood looking down upon the grotesque shape of Hawksbill Mountain. Not far away to their left rose the rugged profile of Grandfather Mountain, but to the south were the coves and hollows down which waters drained to reach the Catawba.

The army split at this point — another precaution against ambush. Campbell took his Virginians south into Turkey Cove, while the others pushed east to North Cove, where they camped for the night. Charles McDowell rejoined them there with word that Ferguson had retreated to Gilbert Town and was up to no mischief. To mark the good news, McDowell and the other colonels carved their names on a large beech tree.

Saturday dawned: the main army climbed over Linville Mountain, missing the now-famous Linville River falls, and turned south to the head of Paddy Creek. There Campbell, reassured by a courier that no trap was waiting, rejoined them, and together they marched down the creek to the broad Catawba. The route was then eastward past the mouth of Linville River to the broad fields of Quaker Meadows, where Charles and Joseph McDowell made their home. The army was now approximately 400 feet lower than it had been at Sycamore Shoals and some 4,500 feet beneath the Bald of the Roan.

It was as if summer had returned.

Vance and the other Burke County men enjoyed brief visits with their families, and the rest of the men settled down to celebrate their victory over the mountains with a good meal. Some of the cattle saved earlier from raiders of Ferguson were now driven out of hiding and butchered. After the hardships and uncertainties of the five days, it was good to be able to relax on level ground in friendly territory. Word came that Colonel Cleveland and Major Winston were enroute from the Yadkin with a large force, and that was additional excuse to celebrate.

Meanwhile, on the same day the mountaineers emerged from the hills, Ferguson learned of their existence. The two deserters, Crawford and Chambers, reached his camp and it is safe to say they did not understate their information. The proclamation he issued next day referred to "an inundation of barbarians," proof enough that the size of the approaching army lost nothing in the telling. He was also informed of plans for Cleveland to join the army, for he named that scourge of Tories in his broadside next day.

Cleveland needed no call from McDowell or Shelby to bring him into the field. William Lenoir, that careful scribbler, discloses that the Wilkes County men were ordered into action in

September when word was received of a band of Tories on the loose in Burke County. Some 350 men collected, marched up the Yadkin into what is today Caldwell County, moved past Fort Defiance, and turned left over Warrior Mountain to Crider's Fort. They spent the night on the spot where Lenoir High School now stands. Moving on toward Burke County, they halted when word was received that 111 Tories were not far ahead at Little-john's Meeting House. Lenoir was ordered to take a few men and try to pull a Musgrove Mill — fake an attack and then retreat, drawing the enemy into an ambush. But it was no go — the Tories had disbanded and scattered.

Cleveland came up and — as Lenoir told it in his pension application many years later — "the march was resumed until they had avanced considerably farther into Burke County when they joined a regiment from Virginia under Colonel Campbell, and some militia from the northwestern side of the Blue Ridge commanded by Col. Sevier and Col. Shelby, together with the militia of Burke Co. under the command of Col. Charles McDowell."

Joseph Winston, commander of the Surrey County men who marched with Cleveland, traced his ancestry to Yorkshire, England. He was born in Virginia in 1746, and at age sixteen joined a company of rangers operating on the frontier. A few months later his company was ambushed by Indians and he was twice wounded. With a companion he hid until the Indians had moved on. The comrade carried him on his back for three days. They lived on wild berries. Eventually he recovered, but he carried the Indian bullets in his body for the rest of his life.

When war began, he took part in the campaign against the Scots at Moore's Creek Bridge, and marched with Lenoir against the Cherokee towns. With Lenoir and Cleveland, he had just returned from the New River campaign against the Tories when orders came to march to Burke County. His wife, meanwhile, gave birth to three sons. A sister who had a baby of her own tried to divide the burden by suggesting that Mrs. Winston give her one of the three. The lady thought about it and refused: "God has given them to me; He will give me strength to nurse them." One of the sons became a judge, the second a general, and the third the lieutenant governor of Mississippi. The city of Winston-Salem draws the first half of its name from Colonel Winston, and the sword presented him by the state after King's Mountain can be seen today in a museum in old Salem.

Truly, it was not only a land of opportunity but a time for it as well. A man could make of himself almost what he pleased.

Meanwhile, two scouts probed southward for word of Ferguson. Anthony Twitty and Lewis Musick captured Ferguson's cook just as he had finished preparing the major's breakfast. From him they learned that Ferguson was still trying to trap the retreating Clarke coming back from Augusta. Satisfied, they ate the breakfast and released the cook, who complained to his commander about being roughly handled. Ferguson told him that, for once, the barbarians had acted quite civilized.

5

Rain on the Just

The problem was Charles McDowell.

On the march across the mountains the five colonels devised a unique command system. Each night they met in council and made plans for the following day. One of their number was designated officer of the day to implement the decisions made in council. The responsibility was rotated daily.

When Cleveland joined the army in Burke County the system continued despite increasing friction and considerable anxiety. Everyone realized that when push came to shove, a single leader would be better than six or seven. A battle almost demanded an overall commander. According to conventional military protocol, McDowell should get the honor. He was the senior officer present in terms of the date of his commission, and, moreover, the army was operating in his assigned district. Yet only Charles McDowell wanted Charles McDowell in command.

Nothing was done on October 1 as the army marched from Quaker Meadows past High Peak in the South Mountains and camped on a ridge between the mouths of Silver Creek, which runs north to the Catawba, and Cane Creek, which runs south. Next day it rained — the first bad weather since the snowstorm on the Roan. Using the weather as an excuse, the army remained in camp while its leaders wrestled with their problem.

The exact sequence of events has been obscured, perhaps because the colonels wanted to protect Charles McDowell's reputation. They liked him personally and respected his patriotism and courage, and no one wanted to leave a record that might later be misunderstood.

It is now apparent, however, that the army spent two days in camp trying to solve the situation. A decision couldn't be postponed: Gilbert Town was only a day's march away and it was assumed that Ferguson was waiting to do battle there.

Opposition to Colonel McDowell was based almost exclusively on the conviction that he was simply not a good battlefield commander. Andrew Hampton had told the others many times of the carelessness, as he saw it, exhibited by McDowell on the night Noah Hampton was murdered. Had enough pickets been out, Hampton insisted, there would have been no surprise attack.

Shelby, who had first-hand experience with McDowell as a commander, considered him too cautious. Cleveland and Winston knew of McDowell's reputation as "an armchair general," and were not impressed. The time for grand strategy had passed.

Various reasons have since been advanced for the rejection of McDowell: his age, his lack of tact, his health. Some of his descendants have even suggested he was overly fond of the bottle and was eliminated for that reason. None of these excuses hold up, however. A bloody battle was ahead and the colonels wanted to make sure the man in command was a fighter. Nothing more.

The showdown came at the council meeting on the afternoon of October 3. It amounted to a face-saving device for McDowell's benefit. Since men from two states were in the army, went the reasoning, it would be logical to ask General Gates — still the commander-in-chief in the South — to name a general officer to command them.

McDowell accepted this theory. What's more he offered to carry a written request to Gates at Hillsborough, where the general was still trying to collect the remains of his "Grand Army." The offer was quickly accepted. The letter was drafted during the evening. It is dated from "Rutherford County, Camp near Gilbert Town," and the date is "October 4, 1780." Addressed to Gates, it says:

> Sir:
>
> We have collected at this place about 1,500 good men, drawn from Washington, Surry, Wilkes, Burk of North Carolina, and Washington County, Virginia, and expect to be joined in a few days by Colonel Williams of South Carolina with about a thousand more. As we have at this place called out Militia without any order from the executives of our different States, and with a view of expelling out of this part of the country the enemy, we think such a body of men worthy of your attention and would request you to send a General Officer immediately to take the command of such troops as may embody in this quarter. Our troops being Militia, and but little acquainted with discipline, we would wish him to be a gentleman of address, and be able to keep a proper discipline without disgusting the soldiery. Every assistance in our power shall be given the Officer you may think proper to take command of us. It is the wish of such of us as are acquainted with General Davidson, and Colonel Morgan (if in service) that one of these Gentlemen may be appointed to this command.
>
> We are in great need of ammunition, and hope you will endeavor to have us properly furnished.
>
> Colonel McDowell will wait on you with this, who

can inform you of the present situation of the enemy, and such other particulars respecting our troops as you may think necessary.

Your most obedient and very able servants,

Benj. Cleveland
Isaac Shelby
John Sevier
Andw. Hampton
Wm. Campbell
Jo. Winston

There are several interesting points about this letter, aside from the emphasis on the selection of a commander who could "keep a proper discipline without disgusting the soldiery." It was two hundred miles to Hillsborough and two hundred miles back, and it is doubtful if the colonels really intended to wait for Gates's decision. Their men had come to "git Ferguson," not to become part of a long campaign. But no one could tell what might happen in a war, and events might require additional time. In that case, an officer such as Davidson or Morgan could be useful.

Davidson was thirty-four years old, from Rowan County. He had fought in New Jersey, winning a battlefield promotion at Germantown. He arrived too late at Charleston to be captured but had been wounded in the summer of 1780 at a skirmish on the Yadkin. A man who understood militia, he was valuable to Continental officers such as Gates and Nathaniel Greene. His death at Cowan's Ford the following year was a serious loss. The Continental Congress voted to build a monument to his memory, and, 122 years later, in 1903, it was erected. A college and a county in North Carolina were named for Davidson as well as a county in Tennessee.

Morgan, of course, was the teamster who received a lashing from a British officer while serving under Braddock in 1755. Since then he had become legendary as the "Old Wagoner,"

serving brilliantly at Quebec and Saratoga. The soldiers loved
him, but the politicians and those officers who played politics
were reluctant to recognize his ability. In disgust, Morgan went
home, which explains why the colonels were unsure if he was in
service. Actually, the fall of Charleston caused him to forget his
personal grievances and return to the field. Belatedly, Congress
promoted him to brigadier general.

But the mountain men had no intention of waiting on either
Davidson or Morgan. As soon as Charles McDowell was on his
way to Gates, another council meeting was held and Campbell
was selected to command. Shelby took the lead in making the
arrangement, pointing out that Campbell was the only officer
from out of state, that he commanded the largest detachment,
and that his men had traveled the greatest distance.

The colonels accepted the argument, but retained the right to
set policy at the daily council meetings. In effect, they simply
appointed Campbell to serve as permanent officer of the day,
instead of rotating the responsibility.

With Major Joseph McDowell taking command of the Burke
County men, the problems on the officer level seemed to have
been solved. But morale had suffered during the long wrangle,
and something was needed to improve the spirits of the rank
and file. Before breaking camp on October 4, the men were
drawn up in a large circle with the officers in the center. News
that "Old Round-About," as Cleveland was known, was going
to speak aroused keen interest. According to John Spelts, a member of McDowell's company, he said something to this effect:

> Now, my brave fellows, I have come to tell you the
> news. The enemy is at hand, and we must up and at
> them. Now is the time for every man of you to do his
> country a priceless service — such as shall lead your
> children to exult in the fact that their fathers were the
> conquerors of Ferguson. When the pinch comes, I
> shall be with you, but if any of you shrink from shar-

ing in the battle and the glory, you can now have the opportunity of backing out and leaving — and you shall have a few minutes for considering the matter.

Major McDowell, the highly respected veteran of a dozen fights, put a question to the men:

"What kind of story will you, who back out, have to relate when you get back home?"

Shelby spelled it out:

"You who desire to decline, will, when the word is given, march three paces to the rear."

The men looked at each other, grinned smally, and waited. Soon the order was given. No one moved. Now the grins were broad and applause began and circled the ring. The men were proud of themselves and of each other.

"When we encounter the enemy," said Shelby, "don't wait for the word of command. Let each one of you be your own officer and do the best you can. If in the woods, shelter yourself and give them Indian play. The moment the enemy gives way, be on the alert and strictly obey orders."

Such men as these needed no detailed instructions and probably would have ignored any given. Shelby was content to speak in general terms; the men knew how to fight the type of battle he described. A lot, of course, would depend on chance, and on the actions of Patrick Ferguson.

The advance began, and the men marched down Cane Creek with its many curves. They were prepared for battle, but they had not gone far when Jonathan Hampton, the club-footed son of Andrew Hampton, came into camp with news that Ferguson had pulled out of Gilbert Town several days earlier in an effort to intercept Colonel Clarke. Where had he gone? That, said Hampton, was the question. The army camped that night at

Gilbert Town in considerable doubt as to what to do next. But then word came in — Ferguson was retreating southward to the British post of Ninety-Six.

The information came from Brigadier General James Williams — and the information was inaccurate. Deliberately inaccurate.

2

James Williams was born in Virginia in 1740, the son of Welsh parents who died when he was young. The boy moved to eastern North Carolina, where he had relatives, and, despite a nose so large his men later joked they treed a possum in it, he married a Miss Clarke. Of medium height and dark complexion, he put on a lot of weight and was considered "corpulent" by age forty.

Three years before the Revolution began, he took his wife and eight children to South Carolina, where he became a farmer, miller and merchant in Laurens County. The war offered him an opportunity to rise about his station, and he became a loyal patriot. As a captain under Williamson, he took part in the campaign against the Cherokees in 1776. Returning home a hero, he was promoted to lieutenant colonel. In the next four years he took part in several minor battles, but his moment of glory came after the victory at Musgrove Mill, where he commanded the left wing. As previously recounted, he took the prisoners captured at Musgrove Mill to Hillsborough and was made a brigadier general by Governor Rutledge of South Carolina.

Taking his new rank to the guerrillas commanded by Colonel Thomas Sumter, Williams tried to take charge. Sumter and his officers refused to accept the new general as their superior. A delegation of officers was selected to advise Governor Rutledge of the reasons why. The governor solved the situation by promoting Sumter to *senior* brigadier general on October 6. By then it really didn't matter.

Undaunted, Williams took his commission to North Carolina and persuaded the governor there to give him permission to organize a corps of one hundred mounted men. On September 23, he issued his call for recruits, promising "beef, bread and potatoes" as an inducement. Allegedly a number of Tar Heels who had shirked duty under their own officers saw in Williams a chance to do some looting. In any case, the men he signed up soon proved they knew how to fight.

With a band of seventy men, Williams marched toward the Catawba and ran into Sumter's little army. The "Carolina Gamecock" was away setting Governor Rutledge straight, and his men were commanded by Colonels Edward Lacey and William Hill. Once more Williams read his commission and tried to take charge, but was told by Hill to get the hell out of camp. Williams, miffed, made camp a short distance away.

Shortly thereafter a courier came in with news that the mountain men were out in force and were chasing Ferguson. Hill and Lacey decided they should find a way to cooperate with Williams, and proposed that their combined forces be split into three division under separate commanders but with all the officers determining the order and movement of the corps. Colonels William Graham and Frederick Hambright, who with sixty men from Lincoln County, North Carolina, had joined the gathering, would compose one unit; Williams and his North Carolina volunteers would be the second company; and the South Carolinians under Lacey and Hill would be the third.

Williams at first refused to have anything to do with the plan unless he could be in overall command, but after some more plain talking from Hill he accepted it.

The opportunity to play the hero again was, however, too good to miss. He dashed off a letter to General Gates which was obviously intended to lay the basis for later claims if circumstances justified. Much of the information in the letter was inaccurate, even including the location from which it was written. Williams dated it, "Burke County, Oct. 2d, 1780," and stated:

Sir:

I am at present about seventy miles from Salisbury, in the fork of the Catawba, with about four hundred and fifty horsemen, in pursuit of Col. Ferguson. On my crossing the Catawba River, I dispatched to different quarters for intelligence, and this evening I was favoured with this news which you may depend upon: That Col. Clarke, of the State of Georgia, with one hundred riflemen, forced his way from South Carolina to Georgia. On his route thither, being joined by seven hundred men, he proceeded to the town of Augusta, and has taken it with a large quantity of goods; but not finding it prudent to continue there, he has retreated to the upper parts of South Carolina, in Ninety-Six district, and made a stand with eight hundred brave men. This moment another of my expresses is arrived from Cols. McDowell and Shelby; they were on their march, near Burke County Court House, with fifteen hundred brave mounted men, and Col. Cleveland was within ten miles of them with eight hundred men, and was to form a junction with them this day.

I expect to join them tomorrow, in pursuit of Ferguson, and under the direction of heaven I hope to be able to render your honor a good account of him in a few days.

I am, &c.,
JAMES WILLIAMS

Once before Williams had taken the credit and reaped the benefit of a mountaineer victory — so why not again? Especially since heaven was directing him.

At the same time this self-serving message was sent to Gage, Williams sent another courier in search of the mountain men. His boast of being in command of a thousand men was noted in the letter McDowell carried to Gage. Obviously, Williams sensed that big things were about to happen, and he was preparing to take as much of the credit as possible.

Unaware of this backwoods intrigue, the little army in its three divisions moved up and into the southern edge of Rutherford County. There on October 4 they were visited by Colonel McDowell en route to Hillsborough. He gave specific information as to the location of the mountain men, and suggested they join them.

Next morning another visitor arrived — an elderly man well known to some of the South Carolinians as a patriot. His name has been lost to history, but he reported he had penetrated Ferguson's camp and had a chat with the major himself. Ferguson told him, he said, that messages had been sent to Cornwallis advising him of the advance of the Backwater Men and asking for help from Tarleton. Pending "Bloody Ban's" arrival, he would find himself a nice-sized hill and wait there — defying the Almighty and all the Rebels out of hell to drive him off. He was tired of running from a bunch of *banditti.*

This was good information and Colonel Hill, after thinking about it, decided it should be given to the mountaineers as soon as possible. Seeking confirmation from the other officers, he discovered that Williams had mysteriously disappeared, leaving his men behind. A little detective work and it was learned that Williams had vanished in the direction of Gilbert Town. Hill shrugged, assuming Williams was just trying to be the first with the news.

It was after sundown before Williams returned. Hill and the other officers asked him where he had been. Williams stalled at first but apparently decided a clean breast of it might help his purpose. He had, he said, been to see the mountain men and had found them on the march south of Gilbert Town. They had arranged, he continued, for the two armies to meet further south at Lawson Fork on the road to the British outpost of Ninety-Six.

Stunned, Hill protested that such a movement would take both armies away from Ferguson who, after feinting south, had turned east toward Charlotte and Cornwallis. Williams didn't argue the point.

It boiled down to an attempt by Williams to use the mountain men for his own purposes. If he could trick them into bypassing Ferguson and capturing Ninety-Six, the whole area of upper South Carolina would become a happy hunting ground for Williams and his volunteers. All the rich Tories hitherto protected by the British would be at their mercy.

While implying this to Hill and Lacey, Williams officially argued that it was the business of South Carolinians to fight first for their own state, and if they could trick some outsiders from beyond the mountains into helping them, so much the better.

This appeal to state pride and self-interest didn't wash. The South Carolinians were professional soldiers after having campaigned for months with Sumter, and they knew that the ultimate safety of their state depended on what happened to the British army. To bypass Ferguson and strike at Ninety-Six would be but to repeat on a larger scale Clarke's fiasco at Augusta. But strategy aside, Hill suspected baser motives. Years later he left no doubt of his suspicions; he wrote:

"I then used the freedom to tell him that I plainly saw through his design which was to get the army into his own settlement, secure his remaining property, and plunder the Tories."

Hurriedly Hill, whose arm was in a sling from a wound he had received some days earlier, hunted up Colonel Lacey and informed him of the danger that Ferguson might escape. Hill explained that he was unable to ride fast because of his wound, so he suggested Lacey go with all speed to Campbell's camp and correct Williams's story.

Lacey agreed. He borrowed Hill's horse, which was considered to be a "good night traveler," and with a scout for a guide started north. It was well after dark and the trail was hard to find and to keep. Twice they strayed off of it and Lacey cocked his pistol and threatened the guide in the belief he might be a traitor. Each time the guide persuaded him to keep going, and after a journey of some twenty miles they reached the mountaineer camp on Green River and slightly southwest of Gilbert Town.

The pickets were rather skeptical when Lacey identified himself. It was a skeptical hour, just before dawn. They blindfolded the visitor and took him to headquarters. Even there Lacey had to do some hard talking before he was believed. Fortunately, perhaps, Shelby had heard of the manner in which Williams used Musgrove Mill to his personal advantage, and it was not hard to convince him that the gentleman was up to his old tricks. Quickly, Lacey laid out the situation, stressing the fact that Ferguson had sent to Cornwallis for reinforcements. If, he said, Ferguson was to be taken, it would have to be done in the next day or two.

Campbell and his colonels agreed. As a matter of fact, they had spent the night "streamlining" their little army to prepare it for a final dash. Sevier and some of his men were getting worried at the prospect of a plunge deep into South Carolina. It would take them too far from the mountains, they thought, and amount to an invitation to Dragging Canoe to attack the undefended settlement. The news that Ferguson had turned east was welcome, even though the movement closer to Cornwallis increased the immediate danger. Lacey was told to get back to Hill as fast as possible and bring as many men as could be trusted to a rendezvous at a ranch that was to become famous later as Cowpens. Travel by day was faster and Lacey got back to his men about 10 A.M.

In Lacey's absence, Williams had tried for the third time to take over. Passing among the South Carolinians, he had ordered them to mount and ride for Lawson Fork far to the south. Colonel Hill had followed behind, explaining to the men that Lacey was conferring with the mountaineers and ordering them to wait until he returned. Upon his return, most of the men mounted and started for the cowpens. Williams and his detachment of seventy men trailed along behind, apparently realizing that safety depended on proximity if not cooperation. The two groups of patriots exchanged obscenities as they marched along, and occasionally tossed a few rocks at each other.

The decision to streamline the main army was based on the new importance of speed and the fact that Ferguson's force had dwindled to not more than one thousand men. Before learning of the approach of the Backwater Barbarians, as he termed them, he had sent some Tory detachments home to avoid feeding them, and had declined to accept others who wanted to join. All were supposed to come back if needed, however, and the purpose of his proclamation and the "roughest Saxon" it contained — to quote his biographer — was to recall them. Several detachments had formed and were moving about hunting for the major even as were his enemies. Indeed, one reason for stopping on King's Mountain was to allow them a chance to find him.

Meanwhile, more reinforcements had joined the Patriots. Thirty men from Clarke's expedition came in, and twenty men under Major William Chronicle from the South Fork of the Catawba also rode up on fresh horses. It seemed safe to cull the army then, leaving behind all footmen and all sick men and horses. Captain Lenoir considered the decision a "proper method to select soldiers, for if any man had a good horse and was any ways bashful, there were others ready to beg for the privilege of taking his place, and his horse, and going."

Lenoir had a horse, but his company was composed of footmen. They, along with the other unmounted, were left under the command of Major Joseph Herndon of Wilkes County, who was ordered to bring them along as fast as possible. Lenoir rode to battle as "a common soldier," free to satisfy his curiosity as he pleased. Among other things, he made an actual body count of the mounted men. Stationing himself at the head of the column, he counted everyone who passed. In view of the controversy that later arose, this was indeed a public service.

"From the best calculations I could make," Lenoir wrote later, "our aggregate was 700."

The area around the cowpens had long been used as a free

119

range. Herds of cattle belonging to various farmers grazed there with the pens used for branding and to separate cattle for purposes of sale. Originally, a man named Hannah built them, but on October 6, 1780, they were owned by a rich Tory named Hiram Saunders. Incidentally, the town of Cowpens is some distance away and draws its name from the fame that attached itself to the cow concentration camp.

The two bodies of troops rode steadily all day and converged on the cowpens early in the evening. Saunders was in bed and insisting he was ill, but the troops pulled him out and questioned him. He knew nothing about Ferguson, he said, having seen neither hide nor hair of him. The men could look if they didn't believe him for sign of an army's passage. They looked and agreed that the Tory, for once, was telling the truth.

While some men were looking, others were hastily killing and roasting a few of Saunders's cows. A field of corn was ravaged too, and a hasty meal was managed by most of the troops. Lacey and Graham culled their men, selecting the best horses. Reluctantly Williams followed suit, obviously hating to see his command shrink to less than fifty men. Altogether, about two hundred were picked for the road, making a strike force of approximately nine hundred men, with at least as many footmen in reserve. (Lenoir estimated the reserve at 1,500 men, but these he didn't count.) But the big question remained: Where was Ferguson? He just had to be around there somewhere.

3

Major Ferguson had been very active after issuing his "pissing proclamation." Not very many Tories had accepted his challenge to prove their manhood, but he was confident many would come in soon. He had sent an express to Cornwallis asking for reinforcements, and Tarleton's dragoons were expected at any hour. (According to Lord Rawdon, none of these messengers got through to Charlotte, but of this the major was blissfully unaware.) A similar appeal for aid had been sent to Colonel J. H. Cruger, British commander of Ninety-Six. Cruger replied immediately, his letter reaching Ferguson two days later. It was like a dash of icy water in the face. Cruger said he had no men to spare. Furthermore, he noted, if the Backwater Men were out in such numbers as Ferguson had described, "I don't see how you can possibly defend the country and the neighborhood you are now in. The game from the mountains is just what I expected."

Perhaps. But to Ferguson they were "a set of mongrels" from which he was too proud to run. Some writers have speculated that jealousy of Tarleton — the dashing, brutal cavalry leader of whom Cornwallis was fond — was at the root of his refusal to accept Cruger's appraisal of his situation. Tarleton, while younger, had been promoted and mentioned in dispatches. Opportunities for new glory were given him almost routinely, while Ferguson operated alone on the frontier with unreliable allies who wavered according to the latest rumor. A proud man was Ferguson, and he had no intention of scurrying into Charlotte with his tail between his legs no matter how many Backwater Men came after him. Ironically, perhaps, he had been promoted to lieutenant colonel, but the news had not yet reached him from England. Conceivably, it might have made a difference had he known, but, given his temperament, it is doubtful.

Lieutenant Allaire, whose account is the best of the several available, gives this record of those crucial days:

> Monday [October] 2d. Got in motion at four o'clock in the afternoon; forded Broad River; marched four miles; formed line of action and lay on our arms. This night I had nothing but the canopy of heaven to cover me.
>
> Tuesday 3d. Got in motion at four o'clock in the morning; marched six miles to Camp's Ford of Second Broad River, forded it and continued on six miles to

one Armstrong's plantation on the banks of the Sandy
Run. Halted to refresh; at four o'clock got in motion,
forded it; marched a mile further and halted near one
Tate's plantation. John West came in camp, is a hundred and one years of age, is amazingly strong in every
sense.

On Wednesday, October 4, Ferguson did not move. His men
rested while scouts sought information as to the enemy's whereabouts. On the day following, he sent this message to Lord
Cornwallis:

> A doubt does not remain with regard to the intel-
> ligence I sent your Lordship. They are since joined
> by Clarke and Sumter — of course are become an ob-
> ject of some consequence. Happily their leaders are
> obliged to feed their followers with such hopes, and
> so to flatter them with accounts of our weakness and
> fear, that, if necessary, I should hope for success
> against them myself; but numbers compared, that
> must be doubtful.
>
> I am on my march toward you by a road leading
> from Cherokee Ford, north of Kings Mountain. Three
> or four hundred good soldiers, part dragoons, would
> finish the business. *Something must be done soon.*
> This is their last push in this quarter, and they are
> extremely desolate and cowed.

A strange blend of pride and caution describes this message.
On the one hand "something must be done soon," and, on the
other, "they are extremely desolate and cowed." The hint about
dragoons was as far as his pride would permit him to go. Obviously, he wanted help from Tarleton. There was no way for him
to know that Tarleton had been ill with malaria for two weeks,
and that Cornwallis himself was incapacitated by a feverish
cold. The earl was later to maintain that he asked Tarleton to

ride but Tarleton, pleading weakness from his fever, declined. Why didn't Cornwallis *order* his subordinate to move? There's no answer to that except, perhaps, the possibility that the commanding general simply underestimated Ferguson's danger and didn't want to inconvenience his favorite cavalry colonel. In any case, the Inspector General of Militia was left to depend upon his militia and upon about one hundred picked "provincials" from New York and New Jersey regiments. These latter were not "regulars" officially, but long service and good training had made them proud and capable.

For Friday, October 6, Allaire made this entry in his diary:

> Got in motion at four o'clock in the morning and marched sixteen miles to Little King's Mountain where we took up our ground.

The King's Mountain range stretches across the line between the two Carolinas at an angle. The North Carolina end reaches toward the east and the South Carolina end to the west. It is roughly sixteen miles long, and only the portion in North Carolina deserves to be called a mountain. A peak named "the Pinnacle" does stand rather conspicuously above the flat countryside, but it is six miles northeast of the ridge Ferguson elected to defend. The range of hills got its name, so legend says, from a man named King who lived at its foot some years before George III assumed the throne. Unaware of local history, Ferguson seems to have considered the mountain's name as some sort of symbol of good fortune. It was King's Mountain, more or less, and he would hold it for his king.

Apart from the name, it is difficult to comprehend why Ferguson was so impressed with the hill. It is but one of several elevations of about the same size, and it rises only sixty feet above the level plain some two miles inside South Carolina. There are two springs at the bottom of the hill, and the water is clear and cool. The ridge itself is about six hundred yards long from base to base and relatively narrow. The rounded top is clear of trees and is about four hundred yards long and from twenty to forty yards wide. It is shaped like a boot pointing northeast with the heel being several feet higher than the rest. The sides of the ridge are fairly steep and now, as then, heavily wooded.

Late in the afternoon of October 6, Ferguson moved his men and supply wagons to the ridge and made camp on the lower, broader "foot" at the point where the toes should begin. He placed his wagons in a semicircle with the open end facing up the foot, and that was the only gesture toward fortifications that he made. His satisfaction was reflected in another express to Lord Cornwallis which said in part:

> I arrived today at Kings Mountain & have taken a post where I do not think I can be forced by a stronger enemy than that against us.

4

The Patriots' stay at the cowpens lasted about an hour. Some of the men were still eating when Joseph Kerr, master spy, appeared. It was as if the prayers of the Reverend Doak invoking the aid of the Almighty were still viable, for Kerr brought the information so desperately needed.

A cripple from infancy, Kerr was born in 1750 in Pennsylvania. His parents moved to the Charlotte area of North Carolina when he was still a child. With the coming of the Revolution, Kerr wanted to make a contribution. Because of his condition he couldn't bear arms and march so he went to the camp of Colonel Charles McDowell in 1780 and offered to become a spy. McDowell liked his spirit and sent him to South Carolina to keep an eye on Cornwallis. Posing as a beggar, Kerr was able to gain access to various enemy camps and come away with much useful information as to the numbers of men and the state of their morale. When McDowell fled across the mountains after Camden, Kerr continued to supply information to any Patriot commander he could find.

His appearance at the cowpens was unexpected but very welcome. Major McDowell and others vouched for him and for his information, which was only six hours old. At noon that day, he said, Ferguson stopped to eat at a plantation only six miles from King's Mountain. His troop strength still numbered less than 1,500 men.

It was good information, confirming as it did the intelligence brought in earlier by the elderly citizen who may have been named John West. Orders were passed to break camp immediately. Campbell decided to send out other scouts to pinpoint Ferguson's location. Major Chronicle, he of the South Fork of the Catawba, nominated one of his men, Enoch Gilmer. But let David Vance tell the story:

> It was objected to because he was not acquainted with the country. Chronicle said that he could find out anything better than those acquainted, for he could act any character that he pleased; that he could cry and laugh in the same breath, and those best acquainted would believe that he was in earnest in both; that he could act the fool so that those best acquainted with him would believe him to be deranged; that he was a shrewd, cunning fellow, and a stranger to fear.
>
> Hence he [Gilmer] was sent among others. He went to a Tory's house on Ferguson's trail and stated to him that he had been waiting on Ferguson's way from Twitty's Ford to Ninety-Six, but missed finding him; that he wished to join the army. The Tory replied that after Ferguson had crossed the river at Twitty's Ford, he had received an express from Lord Cornwallis for him to join the main army at Charlotte; that he [Cornwallis] had called in Tarleton, and would call in his outposts and give Gates another defeat, and reduce North Carolina to British rule as he had South Caro-

lina and Georgia, and would enter Virginia with a larger army than ever had been in America. Gilmer gave this account to the officers.

Kerr also brought news of a large detachment of Tories, perhaps six hundred men, camped only four miles from the cowpens. Obviously it was the major response to Ferguson's appeal and, ordinarily, it would have been a tempting target. But the backwoodsmen hadn't marched so far just to scatter a bunch of Tories; they were after Ferguson and nothing was going to distract them. Campbell was prudent enough, however, to detach Ensign Robert Campbell with eighty volunteers to investigate. The men rode hard, found the Tory camp abandoned, and rejoined the army the next day.

Other sources confirmed the existence of the Tory band, but as far as can be judged it simply melted away on getting news that the Patriots were in the vicinity in force. On paper, at least, it could have created problems for the attackers had it intervened at the right moment, but its leaders decided to play it safe. In any event, its presence didn't delay the Patriot army.

It was about 8 P.M. when the mounted column pulled out of the cowpens and headed east toward the Broad River and King's Mountain. There was no moon, and soon it began to rain. In the blackness, the guides missed their way and some of the men became lost. Campbell's four hundred almost dispersed in the confusion, and with the coming of daylight it was necessary to send men back to round everyone up. Ahead lay the Broad. The possibility that Ferguson's men might be waiting on the east bank to contest the crossing was considered, and Gilmer was sent forward to reconnoiter Cherokee Ford. The advance guard lay hidden in the hills next to the river.

The rain fell steadily. The men had long before been told to wrap their guns with blankets or shirts to keep them dry, and at this point a check was made to be certain the weapons would fire if necessary.

It wasn't necessary. Soon the Patriots heard Gilmer singing "Barney-Linn," "a favorite black-guard song," as Vance put it, and a signal that the road ahead was clear. The crossing began, Thanks to the rain, the river was higher than normal, but no rider got ducked. Once across, Gilmer was sent ahead again to spy out the land. The officers rode at the head of the column and rode slowly — not sure of where Ferguson might be. The men — most of whom had been in the saddle almost continually for twenty-four hours — began to grumble about the slow pace. Vance reported that the men cursed a lot and suggested that if they were going to have a battle to do so and get done with it.

In addition to being tired, the men were still hungry. "When we came to a cornfield," wrote Vance, "it was soon pulled. The soldiers would cut part of the raw corn off the cob, and haul the remainder to their horses." Some three miles beyond Cherokee Ford they stopped briefly for a meal. Some men were better prepared than others. Abram Forney, a private from Lincoln County, managed to cook a cow-bag — udder — which was all that remained of a cow slaughtered the night before. Along came his immediate commander, Major Chronicle.

"Well, Abram," said the major, "you always have something good to eat. I believe I must join you."

Forney made him welcome and was proud later that he did.

The rain started in again and the men were half naked, using their dry clothing to keep their rifles dry. According to Shelby, his brother officers reluctantly concluded that a halt to wait for better weather was necessary. Campbell, Sevier and Cleveland rode up to him, he said, and informed him of their decision. Shelby said he replied:

"By God, I will not stop until night, if I follow Ferguson into Cornwallis' lines."

Without a word, the three officers returned to their respective commands and the march continued. Not more than a mile later, they found a Tory who reported that Ferguson was seven miles ahead and motionless. Encouraged, the men stopped grumbling. And suddenly the rain slackened, then stopped. The

127

sun broke through the clouds and a cool breeze began to blow. It was surely a "sign," declared some of the Presbyterians. The prayers of Reverend Doak were working still.

A couple of miles fell away beneath the tired feet and two of Sevier's men stopped at a house in quest of information. The men at the dwelling were cautious — saying only that the British army wasn't very far away. But a girl followed them out.

"How many are there of you?" she asked.

"Enough to whip Ferguson if we can find him," the men replied.

"He's on that mountain," said the girl, pointing to the wooded ridge some three miles away.

Just beyond the house the officers spied Gilmer's horse tied to a gate. They spurred their horses and came galloping up. Gilmer was inside the house, eating a hearty meal. The Patriots decided to have some fun. Striding in, Campbell declared:

"We have you, you damned rascal."

"A true King's man, by God," said Gilmer, playing his part, happily unaware that he would die in battle before the sun set.

Campbell produced a rope with a running noose on it, and draped it around the spy's neck. Gilmer went into his celebrated act, crying and begging for mercy. The women who had been feeding Gilmer joined in with a torrent of tears. Campbell swore loudly that they would hang him from the gate. Chronicle objected. To do so would be wrong, he said, because the man's ghost would haunt the women's house forever. Campbell agreed. The hanging would take place at the first convenient tree. Gilmer was led out, the rope still around his neck, and taken down the road until he was out of sight. Then the jokers became serious. What news, they asked?

There was plenty. The younger of the women had been to Ferguson's camp that very morning to take him some chickens. The camp was on a ridge between two branches. Deer hunters had camped at the exact place the previous year.

This drew a reply from Major Chronicle. The deer hunters

referred to had been Chronicle and Captain John Mattocks. He remembered the ridge very well.

Chronicle was a native of the area, having been born and raised near Armstrong's Ford on the South Fork of the Catawba. Only twenty-five years old, he was very popular with his men and displayed a quick intelligence that had already won the respect of Sevier and Shelby. Now he and Mattocks — a heavy-weight who was locally famous for a knockout punch — drew apart from the others and compared notes. They returned to say that it would be a simple matter to surround Ferguson — if there were enough men to do it. The idea was instantly approved — since the men would be shooting uphill there would be no danger of hitting each other with the long-range power of their Dickert rifles. Without stopping, the officers began making plans — who would go where.

Suddenly a slight hitch developed. As David Vance told it:

> The last whose duty was to be prescribed was Col. Wm. Graham with his men, who desired leave of absence, alleging that he had received certain intelligence that his wife was dying with the colic, about sixteen miles off near Armstrong's Ford on the South Fork. Campbell stated to him that should be the greatest inducement for him to stay, that he could carry the news — and that if we were successful, it would be to her as good as a dose of medicine.
>
> Graham exclaimed, "Oh, my dear, dear wife! Must I never see her again."
>
> Campbell turned to Chronicle and said angrily: "Shall Colonel Graham have leave of absence?"
>
> Chronicle replied: "It is woman's business; let him go."
>
> Campbell told Graham he might go. Graham said he must have an escort. Chronicle told him he might have one. Graham chose David Dickey. Dickey said

he'd rather be shot in battle than go. Chronicle said, "Dave, you must go."

Dickey said he'd rather be shot on the spot, "but if I must go, I must go, I must."

Graham and Dickey immediately took to the woods and disappeared. Campbell then mentioned to Chronicle that as Graham had gone you [Chronicle] must take his place. Turning to Col. Hambright, Campbell asked: "Have you any objections?" He replied that it was his wish, as Chronicle best knew the ground. Whereupon Chronicle called: "Come on, my South Fork boys," and took the lead.

A few minutes later a lone rider was spotted hightailing it from the ridge where Ferguson waited. Hambright, a native of Germany but a long-time resident of Pennsylvania and North Carolina, recognized the rider as a youth named John Ponder. Aware that Ponder's brother was a notorious Tory, he ordered the young rider's capture. A dispatch to Cornwallis yet again requesting aid was found. The boy supplied additional information of immediate interest: Ferguson, he said, was wearing a checked shirt in the manner of a duster over his glittering uniform. Hambright, his heavy accent no embarrassment, told the men around him:

"Well, poys, when you see dot man mit a pig shirt on over his clothes, you may know who him is and mark him mit your rifle."

It was midafternoon. The sun shone warmly now and the hill ahead was half green, half yellow and red. Down here in the flatlands the first killing frost had not fallen and the leaves were still on the oaks and maples. But the hunt was over, the quarry was at hand.

In silence the men from Watauga and the Holston, from the Yadkin and the Catawba, took their assigned position. The order was passed:

"Fresh prime your guns."

The countersign was "Buford."

6

The Sword of the Lord

Patrick Ferguson had always felt comfortable on hills. King's Mountain was no exception for him. He established his camp on the northeastern end of the ridge, the broadest part of the "foot." (The hill continues at a downward angle for another two hundred feet and then drops off sharply to the little branch below.) Inside the semicircle of wagons, the tents of his 1,125 men stretched back up the ridge.

His one hundred "Provincials" wore the traditional red coats and white breeches of the British army. They were armed with the old and reliable "Brown Bess" musket, complete with bayonet. Few of the thousand-odd Tories he had trained wore anything resembling a uniform, although most of them had pinned some type of cockade made of cloth or paper to their hats to distinguish them from their similarly-dressed neighbors on the other side. They also had bayonets — of a sort. Ferguson, always the experimentor, had devised a way to make the local "butcher" knives fit into the barrel of a musket. He did this by cutting down the handles. The practice was to load and fire until the enemy got close. Then one stuck in the "bayonet" and charged.

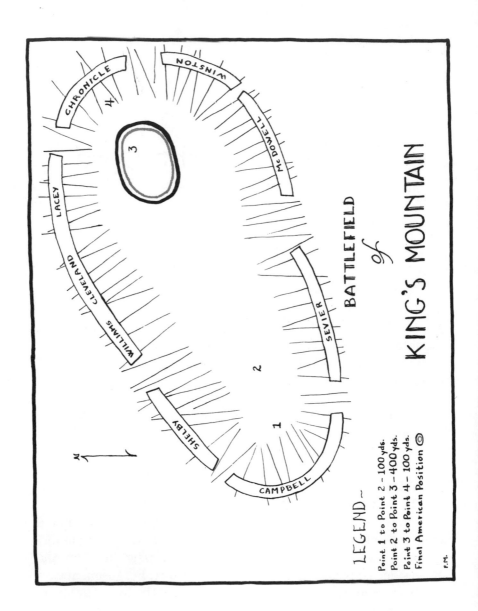

LEGEND ~

Point 1 to Point 2 – 100 yds.
Point 2 to Point 3 – 400 yds.
Point 3 to Point 4 – 100 yds.
Final American Position ⊚

BATTLEFIELD
of
KING'S MOUNTAIN

F.M.

It was a bit inconvenient, perhaps, since the gun couldn't be fired until the knife was removed, but as a practical matter the soldier wasn't going to do much shooting at close range anyway. More important was the advantage he obtained in having cold steel available in a melee where the rebel opposing him could only use his gun as a club.

That Ferguson, the best shot in the British army and the inventor of a breechloading rifle, should be reduced to using such primitive weapons as a converted butcher knife in a defensive battle against the sharpshooters of the hills, is proof enough of his submission to the conventional military wisdom of the day. Had his old rifle corps from Brandywine, armed with the Ferguson Rifle, been present on King's Mountain, both the tactics employed and the outcome might have been much different.

But Ferguson had adjusted. Now his hopes for advancement lay not in some strange new weapon and revolutionary techniques, but in the attempt to recast loyal Americans into reasonable imitations of the disciplined redcoat. In the belief that he had succeeded, he settled down on King's Mountain instead of marching on to Charlotte and safety. With him were his cook, his mistresses, and at least two officers in whom he had confidence: Captains Abraham dePeyster of New York, and Alexander Chesney of South Carolina.

It had been a quiet day. The men had rested in their tents until the rain stopped, and after that had dried out in the sunlight. It was good to relax. As an unknown poet put it:

> 'Twas on a pleasant mountain
> the Tory heathens lay
> With a doughty Major at their head,
> one Ferguson, they say
> Cornwallis had detached him
> a thieving for to go
> And catch the Carolina men
> or lay the Rebels low

Captain Chesney mounted his horse in midafternoon and made the rounds of the pickets stationed in the woods at the bottom of the hill. All reported no signs of the Rebels. The inspection completed, the officer rode back to the camp and was dismounting preparatory to reporting to Ferguson that all was peaceful, when a shot rang out in the woods below the hilltop.

"I immediately paraded the men and posted the officers," Chesney reported later. But then, some minutes after the first shot, he was wounded and his horse killed by a volley.

With no more warning than that the battle was on.

From the north side of the hill came an Indian war whoop, and then a lot of them. DePeyster was troubled. He turned to Ferguson and commented:

"Things are ominous. Those are the same yelling devils I fought at Musgrove Mill."

Before being wounded, Chesney had extended the militia (the British used the word too) in a straight line up the crest of the hill — from the camp near the "toes" to the narrow, higher "heel" on the southwestern end of the ridge. Ferguson, using a silver whistle as a signal, kept his "provincials" as a mobile reserve, rushing them from one side of the hill, from one end of the hill, to the other, as danger threatened. Mounted on a white horse, he dashed back and forth as needed, an inspiring sight. His men responded well to his commands. They had been long trained, most of them, and they believed in Ferguson, perhaps because he believed in them.

As the war whoops grew louder and the sound of firing spread all along the ridge, they needed all the faith they could muster. The enemy seemed invisible, flitting like shadows from tree to tree. And when, occasionally, they found a target down the hill, they tended to overshoot.

2

The Patriots' march had ended about a half mile from the southwestern end of the hill. Horses were tied, and personal gear such as blankets were stored. Weapons were checked. The colonels commanding formed the men into four columns, the two on the left assigned to positions along the northern side of the hill, and the two on the right moving around the end of the ridge to the southern side.

Chronicle on the extreme left and Winston on the extreme right went first, since they had the greatest distance to travel to reach their stations on the far northeastern end of the ridge. The rest of the men waited silently as the first troops moved out on horseback.

Cleveland, commander of the northern flank, moved out next. Under his orders were Lacey and James Hawthorn, who had replaced the wounded Hill. Williams, largely ignored by the leaders and despised by all except his handful of men, tagged along behind Cleveland.

On the far right, meantime, Joseph McDowell led the Burke County men to the area of the "little toe." Sevier was behind him, taking up position along the arch of the "foot." Finally the two "center" lines — Shelby on the left, Campbell on the right — semicircled the "heel."

As the detachments advanced, scouts went ahead to silence the pickets. Several were eliminated, giving all troops more time to reach their positions, but one man close to the hill fired wildly as through the underbrush he spotted moving figures. Immediately, from the top of the hill came the roll of drums and the piercing blast of a silver whistle. Tories formed a line along the crest and opened fire on Shelby's men. The muskets did no harm at that distance, but some of the hillbillies became annoyed and felt their dignity demanded return of the fire. Shelby ordered them to press on to their assigned places before blazing back. As always, the standing order was:

"See what you shoot and shoot what you see."

Meanwhile, having the shortest distance to travel, Campbell rounded the southwestern edge of the hill. He stripped off his coat, waved his sword, and commanded:

"Shout like hell and fight like devils."

It was then the war whoops that dePeyster thought so ominous began ringing through the trees, and the Virginians charged up the hill. Ferguson rushed his Provincials to the scene and as the Patriots neared the top he ordered a bayonet charge. Some of Campbell's men tarried too long, and when at last they turned to run the retreat was almost a rout. Lieutenant Allaire, mounted on a horse, claimed to have used the advantage given by his mount to cut down a Rebel captain who was on foot with "one blow of my sword."

Near the bottom of the hill, the British stopped as Ferguson's whistle shrilled a signal. On the northern side of the "heel" Shelby's men were climbing. Hurriedly, the Provincials rushed back uphill to defend against the new threat.

Campbell's troops ran across the hollow at the foot of the hill and reformed on the other side. Then, with Campbell leading, they crossed back the way they had come and started up the hill again. Drury Mathis, a Tory from South Carolina, had been wounded while charging down the mountain, and now lay on his back about halfway down. As the mountaineers returned he pretended to be dead, but managed to observe them. As he told it later, they seemed "like devils from the infernal regions," and were the most powerful men physically he had ever seen: "tall, raw-boned, sinewy, with long matted hair."

Another witness some distance from the battle said that at that stage "the mountain was covered with flame and smoke and seemed to thunder."

While Campbell's men, angry now, were returning, Shelby's troops seesawed down again under the impact of a similar bayonet charge. But they fell back in better order, shooting as they went. Again, the British had to let their advantage go to turn back to the other side of the hill, and just as promptly the men from the lower Holston went back up again.

Ten minutes or so passed in this desperate fashion. Meanwhile, the other detachments were coming into action and, by so doing, took some of the pressure off the heel of the boot.

Cleveland, his 250 pounds astride a giant horse, gave something of a speech as he led his men along. While no one was taking notes, it was remembered later as sounding something like this:

"My brave fellows, yonder is your enemy and the enemy of all mankind. We have beat the Tories before and we can beat them again. They are all cowards. If they had the spirit of men they would join their fellow-citizens in supporting the independence of their country. Fire as quick as you can and stand your ground as long as you can. When you can do no better, get behind trees or retreat, but, I beg, don't run off. If we are repulsed, let us make a point of returning and renewing the fight."

No early bayonet charge was made on Cleveland. His Wilkes and Surrey men moved from tree to rock to tree, climbing steadily and shooting at everything that moved. Cleveland's horse was killed, but he pulled himself erect and led the way on foot. Above the rifle fire could be heard his shout:

"A little nearer to them, my brave boys; just a little nearer."

Meanwhile, Winston's column was encountering difficulty in reaching its assigned position — an important one because it lay across Ferguson's line of retreat eastward to Charlotte.

William Lenoir, his company of footmen left back at Green River, was something of a free lance. Before the battle he made a pact with two friends, Robert Cleveland and Jesse Franklin, "to stand together and to support each other," but the trio was quickly separated. Since Winston moved out first, Lenoir went along. The men rode far to the right and soon lost sight of their colleagues in the wooded maze. They also lost sight of the ridge on which the enemy waited. Suddenly "an officer came into sight and directed Colonel Winston to dismount and march up the hill — which we did in proper line of battle."

It was the wrong hill. After they had marched a hundred

yards, the officer reappeared and called for Winston. Lenoir answered for him. The officer — whose identity was never learned — then shouted:

"Mount your horses and push on; the enemy is a mile ahead."

The men turned and ran back to their horses, mounted them, "and rode as fast as fox hunters through a rough, brushy woods, crossing hollows and ridges and a brook or two without any guide or pilot and without any knowledge of the position of any other part of the army. We were certainly directed by a Supernatural Power, and arrived at a very advantageous station the very moment the firing began on the other parts of the line. We could not have been placed in better position as to ground by all the men in the world, and our troops proceeded to surround the enemy as soon as possible, sustaining and returning their fire."

On Winston's right at the northeastern end of the hill, the South Fork men under their new commander, William Chronicle, made contact. Robert Henry, a sixteen-year-old, was there:

> "Enoch Gilmer called on Hugh Erwin, Adam Barry and myself to allow him close to the foot of the hill. We marched with a quick step, letting Major Chronicle advance about ten steps before us, but further from the hill than we were, until we met the wing [Winston] from the other side of the hill. Then Chronicle having a military hat . . . clapped his hand to it in front and raised it up and cried, Face to the hill. The words were scarcely uttered when a ball struck him and he dropped; and in a second after, a ball struck William Rabb, about six feet from Chronicle, and he dropped. We then advanced up the hill close to the Tory lines."

Alarmed at this heavy new assault at the opposite end of the battle line, Ferguson ordered dePeyster to take part of the Provincials from the southwest front and meet the challenge. It was an expensive movement along the ridge as from both sides McDowell and Cleveland's men poured in a deadly fire on the moving men. Discipline was such, however, that dePeyster was able to launch a bayonet charge directed primarily at the South Fork men but overlapping on Winston's detachment. Before charging, the British fired a volley. Captain Mattocks was killed. Some of the South Forks men seemed to waver. Lenoir, on their left, saw the confusion and "ran diagonally to those men who had sustained the charge, and encouraged them to load well and make a bold push — which they did."

Thus Lenoir, a captain without a company, found a need for his leadership and met that need without hesitation. In the process he was slightly wounded in his left arm and again in his side. Another bullet "passed through my hair above the tie, without touching the skin."

The youthful Henry was preparing to fire as the British crashed down the steep hillside. He was approached by a soldier with bayonet extended. "I stepped back and was in the act of cocking my gun when his bayonet was running along the barrel and gave me a thrust through my hand and into my thigh. My antagonist and myself both fell. The Fork boys retreated and loaded their guns. I was then lying under the smoke, and it appeared that some of them [the Patriots] were not more than a gun's length in front of the bayonets, and the farthest could not have been more than twenty feet in front when they discharged their rifles. It was said that every one dropped his man. The British then retreated in great haste, and were pursued by the Fork boys."

As the men returned, William Caldwell spotted the wounded Henry and paused beside him to pull the bayonet from his thigh. The steel still hung to Henry's hand. Caldwell, in something of a hurry, gave the hand a kick and went on.

"The thrust gave me much pain," Henry reported, "but the pulling of it was much more severe."

After the bayonet was free, Henry looked for its owner. The British soldier lay dead on the hill. "I suppose that when the soldier made the thrust, I gripped the trigger and discharged her — the load must have passed through his bladder and cut a main artery of his back as he bled profusely."

And now, as Representative Bailie Peyton of Tennessee recounted in a speech to Congress in 1834: "The mountain appeared volcanic. There flashed along its summit and around its base and up its sides, one long sulphurous blaze."

Savage was the struggle. Pent-up bitterness and long-accumulated hatred found an outlet on both sides. Neighbor fired at neighbor, brother at brother, hunting shirt at red coat. It was a scene for poets and in the years that followed many tried to do the battle justice. Some came close:

> What time from right to left
>   there rang the Indian war-whoop wild
> Where Sevier's tall Watauga boys
>   through the dim dells defiled

And there's a glimpse of the burly Cleveland, fighting on foot after his horse was killed and sounding a bit like his alleged ancestor, Oliver Cromwell:

> "Now, by God's grace," cried Cleveland,
>   my noble colonel he,
> Resting to pick a Tory off,
>   quite coolly on his knee

Another anonymous poet described the action very succinctly:

> The morrow's clouds hung low and still
> As up the steep and rugged hill
> A thousand hunters sped;
> With rifles pouring fire and smoke
>   through bayonets they fiercely broke,
>   And piled the ground with dead

The British have even supplied a poem which tells how the battle looked from their position:

> But vain was pluck, and vain each charge
>   for from each tree there came
> A deadly rifle bullet,
>   and a little spurt of flame
> The men who fired we could not see —
>   they picked us off like game

Incidents of individual action were many and a few were reported:

Charles Gordon, one of Cleveland's men, evaded a bayonet thrust, grabbed his enemy by his hair, which was arranged in a queue, and began dragging his victim downhill. The Tory officer pulled a pistol and fired at his captor, the bullet hitting, and breaking, Gordon's left arm. Annoyed, Gordon retaliated with his sword, chopping down his prisoner with one blow. He survived the battle and later married a daughter of William Lenoir. Their descendants live today in Happy Valley.

William Robertson, fighting under Hampton and McDowell, was shot through the body. The bullet went in one side and out the other. Quite naturally Robertson, upon examining his wound, decided he was finished. Next to him on the hill was another man whose weapon had ceased to function. Robertson handed over his rifle and shot bag, and watched them go back into action. Much to his surprise, he lived despite the wound. Meanwhile his brother, Tom, was engaged with a ghost. Someone kept calling his name. Eventually, Robertson peeped out from behind a tree to see who it was. A bullet cut the bark above his head. Instantly Robertson fired — and saw a Tory neighbor fall wounded from his hiding place.

"Robertson, you've ruined me," said the Tory.

"The devil help you," replied the Patriot.

An even closer relationship was involved in another man-to-man duel. A Patriot not otherwise identified noticed that someone was shooting with fatal effect from a position in the Tory lines. He scouted around until he could pinpoint the source of the deadly fire — a hollow chestnut tree. The enemy was firing *through* a knothole in the tree much as he would do if in a fort. With an effort the Patriot put a bullet through the knothole. The firing ceased. After the battle, he came back to the bullet-scarred chestnut. There on the ground behind it he found his Tory brother —dead.

Thomas Young, fighting with Williams, spotted a cousin as he neared the top of the hill. The youth was Matthew McCrary, a reluctant Tory whose mother made him join Ferguson in the hope it would persuade the British not to hang his father, who was a prisoner. Matthew, on seeing Young, whooped with joy and ran down the hill to throw his arms around his cousin. "I told him to get a gun and fight," said Young. "He said he could not. I bade him to let me go that I might fight."

Moses Shelby, brother of the colonel, was shot twice, the second wound knocking him out of the fight. Someone helped him down the hill to the little branch and bandaged his thigh. Soon the captain noticed a soldier making a second visit to the branch for water. "If you come back a third time," said Shelby, "I'll shoot you. This is no time to shirk duty."

Lieutenant Reece Bowen needed no one to remind him of duty. He exposed himself with reckless bravery again and again while fighting with Campbell's men. A friend advised him to hide behind a tree. Bowen refused — his honor, he said, wouldn't permit him to do so. A minute later he was hit in the chest and pitched forward dead. His brother Charles, fighting some distance away, eventually learned of Reece's death and began searching for the body. The search carried him to the East and to the top of the ridge. He saw a Tory wave a white handkerchief. Enraged at the thought that some might escape by surrendering, Bowen shot him down. Then he stepped behind a tree to reload. Cleveland, fighting on foot, saw the stranger and demanded the countersign. Bowen, shocked and bewildered, couldn't think of it. Cleveland leveled his rifle. Bowen grabbed his tomahawk from his belt and charged. Cleveland's gun missed fire and Bowen plowed into him. In an instant he would have killed the colonel, but another soldier grabbed his arm. Belatedly, Bowen remembered the countersign and gasped out "Buford." Cleveland dropped his rifle and embraced the man who had tried so hard to kill him.

3

The key to the next stage of the battle is given in a short report to Lord Cornwallis by Abraham dePeyster. For some reason it has been overlooked by historians. Only recently unearthed by the personnel of King's Mountain National Military Park, it is a dramatic and very important document.

According to dePeyster, his "little detachment" of Provincials "charged the enemy with success and drove the right wing of them back in confusion." This was Shelby, still engaged in the seesaw battle along the "heel" of the ridge. Shelby described the same charge in this fashion:

"In the course of the battle we were repeatedly repulsed by the enemy and driven down the mountain. In this succession of repulses and attacks, and in giving succour to the points hardest pressed, much disorder took place in our ranks: the men of my column, of Campbell's column and a great part of Sevier's, were mingled together in the confusion of the battle. Toward the latter part of the action, the enemy made a fierce and gallant charge upon us from the summit of the mountain, and drove us near to the foot of it. The retreat was so rapid that there was great danger of its becoming a rout."

It might have been a rout but, according to dePeyster, "Unfortunately Major Ferguson made a signal [with his silver whistle] for us to retreat, being afraid that the enemy would get possession of the height from the other side. The militia being ignorant of the cause of our retreat, it threw the few that stood their post under the officers from 96, into disorder . . ."

Those same officers, acording to dePeyster, "cut down" some of their own men in an effort to stop the panic. This drastic measure failed — indeed, given the similarity of the dress and appearance of men on both sides, it probably increased the confusion. The militia unit involved was composed of North Carolina men. Not surprisingly, under the circumstances, they began to move from their positions and "intermix," as dePeyster put it, with the uniformed Provincials who, at least, were recognizable as friends.

The confusion on the crest gave the Patriots time to recover and allowed units on both sides of the "heel" to advance up the hill at the same time. But, mysteriously, a rumor swept the troops that Tarleton was at hand. It stemmed, perhaps, from the shouts and screams on the crest as the British officers tried to save the situation. Unaware of what was happening to the militia, the mountain men interpreted the uproar as a reaction to Tarleton. Sevier had to ride along the line, assuring his men that Tarleton was far away and lucky for him that this was the case. Soon the men were grinning sheepishly, and turning back to the climb with renewed determination.

On the other side of the hill men were also climbing and the two groups reached the open space of the crest at the same moment. The seesaw across the mountaintop had broken down. Sevier and Shelby reached the top almost together as the few remaining defenders of the "heel" withdrew in a panic. Said Sevier to his friend and neighbor:

"By God, they've burned off your hair."

The Provincials at this point, according to dePeyster, had been reduced to "2 sergeants & 20 R & file." With the militia fleeing along the ridge and overrunning the survivors, "we could no longer act."

Now the entire Patriot force of the center — the center columns, that is — composed of men under Shelby, Sevier and Campbell, were crowded together on the heel and driving toward the northeast where the tents and wagons stood. As their triumphant war whoops became louder and louder, the men in the semicircle around the northeastern end of the ridge renewed their attacks and McDowell on the right and Cleveland on the left reached the top along the arch of the foot.

Near the northeast summit, where the steep rise begins to flatten out, Hambright was hit in the thigh as he sat on his horse. The bullet cut an artery, filling his boot with blood. One of his men urged him to dismount for treatment, but he refused. Aware that Chronicle and Mattocks were dead, he feared his withdrawal would discourage the South Fork boys at a critical moment in the battle. Rising in his stirrups, he shouted:

"Huzza, my brave poys, fight on a few minutes more."

"The left," said dePeyster, meaning the troops at the northeastern end of the hill, "on seeing us broke, gave way and got in a crowd on the hill." All efforts to rally the men failed and nothing remained to do "but to make a break through the enemy."

DePeyster thus answers questions much debated by historians — was Ferguson merely continuing the battle, was he deliberately seeking death before dishonor, or was he trying to escape the trap when he made his last charge?

He was trying to escape, says dePeyster.

DePeyster tried to assemble as many men as possible to accompany Ferguson. So did the other officers, he reports. But most of the men were out of ammunition and had no stomach for new adventures. Only four men could be found to follow their leader.

On his great white horse, the slender young man from the Scottish hills charged down the northeastern slope. A hundred feet would get him through the enemy, a hundred yards would see him safely on his way to Charlotte. In his left hand he brandished a sword of Spanish steel on which was engraved Spanish words meaning:

> Draw me not without reason
> Sheathe me not without honor.

For an hour the sharpshooters had been looking for this target. Several claimed to have glimpsed him but he vanished before they could draw bead. Now, however, a dozen rifles were trained on him and the range was short. One ball hit him in the thigh, another reshattered his crippled arm, another found his body. Still he kept his saddle, waving his sword. Robert Young of Sevier's company leveled "Sweet Lips" and fired. Hit in the head but still alive, Ferguson fell from his horse, which galloped on down the hill unchecked.

A simple stone marks the spot today.

Command devolved upon Captain dePeyster and he wasted no time. As he explained in his report to Lord Cornwallis:

> In this situation — the small body of soldiers we had being cut up, and finding it impossible to rally the militia, I thought it proper to surrender as the only means of saving the lives of some brave men still left. In justice to the officers and men I must beg leave to acquaint your Lordship that they behaved with the greatest Gallantry & attention, even to a wish; as to the militia, there were many of them, both officers and men, who, when the enemy was within a hundred yards around us, that behaved with a Degree of Gallantry.

But to decide it was proper was one thing, actually to surrender was something else. There was too much confusion, and too much hatred. As Shelby put it:

> It was some time before a complete cessation of firing on our part could be effected. Our men, who had been scattered in the battle, were continually coming up and continued to fire without comprehending in the heat of the moment what had happened; and some who had heard that at Buford's defeat the British had refused quarter to many who asked it, were willing to follow that bad example.

146

Shelby didn't exaggerate. Despite the white flags, men kept shooting. The shout, "Tarleton's quarter" was heard repeatedly, and a kind of vicarious revenge was obtained on the hapless Tories. Among those who kept firing was Joseph Sevier, eighteen-year-old son of John Sevier, who had heard that his father was dead.

"The damned rascals have killed my father," said the youth, "and I'll keep shooting till I kill every son of a bitch of them."

Only when his father rode up to him with word it was the boy's uncle, Captain Robert Sevier, who was wounded, did Joseph's private battle end. Robert Sevier lived to reach the top of the Blue Ridge once more, but died before reaching home.

Shelby was also trying to stop the killing. Recklessly, he rode between the two groups of men to within fifteen feet of the enemy.

"If you want quarter," he bellowed, "throw down your arms."

The British troops obeyed. They were crowded into a space less than one hundred feet wide and two hundred feet long at the northeast corner of the hill — some eight hundred men still able to stand The mountaineers ringed them, to stare and to taunt. Campbell, his shirt wet with sweat and his red hair gleaming in the sunlight, ordered the prisoners to sit down. Order seemed to return so the official victory cheer was commanded.

Three times this shout rang out:

"Hurrah for LIBERTY."

The noise was like thunder and was heard by residents in the area around the mountain. For an hour they had listened to the sound of guns, wondering how the battle went. Now they knew.

A strange sort of silence followed the cheer as men who had risked their lives and the safety of their families seemed to need time to savor the reality of victory.

And then came the crack of a rifle. Colonel James Williams swayed on his saddle and said to William Moore of Campbell's company:

"I'm a gone man."

Angry and embittered by the "silent treatment" given him before the battle, Williams had swallowed his pride and fought bravely. Thomas Young, a teenage private, had been near Williams at the beginning of the fight and saw his horse shot out from under him. Later Young noticed Williams again, "on top of the mountain, in the thickest of the fight."

Young's statement continued:

> The moment I heard the cry that Colonel Williams was shot, I ran to his assistance for I loved him as a father. They carried him into a tent and sprinkled some water in his face. He revived and his first words were: "For God's sake, boys, don't give up the hill." I left him in the arms of his son, Daniel, and returned to the field to revenge his fate.

That revenge was well underway by the time Young got back. Everyone assumed that a defiant Tory had sneaked a final shot and hit someone. Most of the mountaineers weren't aware that Williams was the target. They knew only that someone had been hit. The old anger flamed and in less than a second they were shooting at the helpless prisoners.

Colonel Campbell, apparently thinking stern action was necessary to keep the prisoners under control, told those nearest to him to fire. One of those men was Lieutenant John Hughes, who in his pension statement years later was quite candid:

"General Williams was mortally wounded, after the British had raised their flag to surrender, by a fire from some Tories. Colonel Campbell then ordered a fire on the Tories and we killed near a hundred of them after the surrender of the British and could hardly be restrained from killing the whole of them."

Hughes was a brave soldier, tall and tigerlike. He was to win lasting frame the next year at Cowpens and go on to a long and respectable life as an elder in the Presbyterian church. So his report has to be accepted, with, perhaps, due allowance for exaggeration in his account of the number of men killed.

Later, after the smoke drifted away from King's Mountain, it was officially decided that the bullet that killed Williams came from a party of foragers returning to the hill. This is absurd on its face — had any group come close enough to pick off Williams, they would surely have been seen. They would have been pursued. And what body of men — be it twenty or two hundred — would have approached so close after a battle lasting an hour had just ended?

The theory of the vanishing forager was put forth, however, to offer an acceptable alternative to a third possibility — that the fatal bullet came from one of the South Carolinians who resented Williams's effort to take command and steal all glory. Such a man might have hoped the Tories would kill Williams in the battle. When this didn't happen, he did it himself and let the Tories be blamed. Such a charge was made by Colonel Hill, the South Carolinian who with Lacey had blocked Williams's scheme to send the mountaineers promenading down to Ninety-Six. Hill was in a position to know, but his accusation is rejected out of hand by Draper, ever the gentleman historian, who states that "for the honor of humanity we are constrained to discard so improbable and unpatriotic a suggestion."

Exactly how the honor of humanity is involved, Draper doesn't say. Why it is noble and patriotic for a man to shoot his neighbor or even his brother in the name of Liberty, but ignoble for him to shoot an officer who tried to misuse his allies for personal glory, is a difficult question to answer.

In death, however, much is forgiven. And even Draper couldn't accept the other extreme — a fable constructed by friends of Williams. They would have it that their hero engaged in personal combat with Patrick Ferguson and cut, or shot, him down, and was, in his turn, shot by the Scot with a pistol as, chivalrously, he dismounted to give aid to his stricken foe. In this version, Williams lived only long enough to know that his individual action turned the tide, and — with the victory shout ringing in his ears — he died, a contented smile upon his manly face.

Shelby, who seems to have kept his head — at least he tells us that he did — once again stopped the slaughter. This time he ordered the prisoners to move away from their weapons, thus depriving any trigger-happy avenger of the excuse of self-defense.

Apparently Campbell had second thoughts about his impulsive order to fire. Shelby has related that on the day after the battle, Campbell sought a private conversation. They stood in the morning sunlight so close they almost touched. Campbell, speaking "in a lower tone of voice than usual, and with a slight smile," said:

"Sir, I cannot account for my conduct in the latter part of the action."

This statement was later to be misconstrued, but it seems obvious today that the Virginian was sorry he had ordered men to fire on disarmed prisoners.

But to return to the day of battle — James Collins, who had fought under Shelby, felt sorry for the enemy. He later wrote:

> After the fight was over, the situation of the poor Tories appeared to be really pitiable; the dead lay in heaps on all sides, while the groans of the wounded were heard in every direction. I could not help turning away from the scene before me, with horror, and though exulting in victory, could not refrain from shedding tears.

Almost the first thought, it seems, of every man from private to colonel was to take a look at the famous Ferguson, who had been carried to the bottom of the hill by the little trickle of water issuing from a spring. Shelby himself rode down to the spot. Thinking the fallen officer still alive, the American addressed him:

"Major, the fatal blow is struck — we've Burgoyned you."

This was a new word coined after General Burgoyne's surrender to Gates at Saratoga. It might have inspired a sharp reply from Ferguson in view of the way Gates's northern laurels changed to southern willows at Camden, had the major been alive to make it.

Robert Henry, despite the pain of his wounded leg and hand, "had a desire" to see Ferguson "and went and found him dead. He was shot in the face and in the breast. It was said he had other wounds. Samuel Talbot turned him over and got his pocket pistol."

Collins also viewed the body, and, businesslike now, saw it as an example of the marksmanship of his colleagues:

> On examining the body of their great chief, it appeared that almost fifty rifles must have been leveled at him at the same time. Seven rifle balls had passed through his body, both his arms were broken, and his hat and clothing were literally shot to pieces. Their great elevation above us had proved their ruin; they overshot us altogether, while every rifle from below seemed to have had the desired effect. In this conflict I had fired my rifle six times, while others perhaps fired nine or ten. . . .

Lieutenant Sam Johnson of Cleveland's regiment was badly wounded and thought to be dying. To honor his last wish, Cleveland and two soldiers carried him to view the fallen Ferguson. Whether it hurt or helped may be debated, but, in any event, Johnson recovered from his wounds.

Elias Powell, a youth born in the vicinity of Crider's Fort, now Lenoir, in Caldwell County, had joined Ferguson's ranks early in the year and become something of a personal orderly. His affection and sense of duty did not diminish with defeat, and it was he who removed the still-breathing officer to the running water and bathed his bloody face. When it was apparent that Ferguson was dead, Powell was shoved aside. Several soldiers stripped the body, dividing up its clothing as trophies of war. Powell had already taken the precaution, however, of removing Ferguson's silver whistle as his own prize.

What followed has its own peculiar logic. The victors, dirty, blood-stained and bearded, began urinating on Ferguson's naked body.

This is the act which Draper asked to be excused "from the pain of recording." This is what Tarleton meant when in his history of the southern campaign he wrote:

"The mountaineers, it is reported, used every insult and indignity, after the action, toward the dead body of Major Ferguson."

And why not? These mountaineers were not professional soldiers, trained to observe a code of warfare, although at times they fought like professionals. They weren't even serving in the capacity of militia, duly called up, equipped, trained, and led by officers assigned to them under the authority of the state. They were volunteers, citizen-farmers, who had answered the call of their natural leaders to repel a danger.

Ferguson was the man who had laid waste much of the western Carolinas, stealing cattle, burning homes, and hanging men he deemed to be traitors. Moreover, Ferguson was the man who had threatened to cross the mountains and carry fire and sword through the settlements on the other side. He had called the Backwater Men "barbarians" and "mongrels," ascribing to them crimes and atrocities he knew they had not committed. Lastly, he had suggested to the Tories of North Carolina that unless they came to arms against these "dregs of mankind," they would be "pissed upon forever and ever" by these same mountain men.

So, since Ferguson had made the suggestion, they pissed cheerfully upon his dead body in the most complete gesture of triumph, of revenge, of contempt, that either they, or he, could have devised. These men had marched for almost two weeks, crossing the most rugged mountain chain in eastern America.

For thirty-six hours they had been without sleep, and for almost twenty-four hours they had eaten only scraps of food. They were still, in the very hour of their triumph, in deadly danger, for they were almost out of ammunition and saddled with an army of prisoners. Cornwallis and the dragoons of Tarleton were at most only thirty miles away and could easily be just over the next hill. The safety of the mountains was days away. Hate had driven them, hate and pride. Ferguson had seen fit to add insult to injury, to make the quarrel between them a personal thing. And there was something more. "Bloody Ban" might be hated for his ruthless ways but, when all was said, he was just another dragoon. Ferguson, with his ability to woo the Tory and to train him, was a deadly threat to American unity and thus to ultimate victory. About that victory these men, who wanted first of all to be left alone, felt strongly, sincerely. All these factors explain — and I believe justify — their final gestures of contempt on Ferguson.

A Scottish proverb says: "War begins when hell opens."

When the point had been made, the men left Ferguson and turned to forage for food, of which there was little enough. Powell, aided by three volunteers, washed the body and wrapped it in a cowhide. Tradition has it that wrapped with it was the body of Virginia Sal, his red-headed mistress, who was killed by a random bullet early in the fight. The bodies were buried in a shallow grave at the foot of the hill. To protect the bones and mark the spot, some stones were piled on top of the raw earth.

In years to come as passions ebbed and it was possible to admire a fallen foe, that pile of stones was enlarged to form a cairn — considered appropriate for a soldier of Scotland. And on the 150th anniversary of the battle, a stone monument was erected over the grave in the name of the citizens of the United States. Of Ferguson it says simply:

A SOLDIER OF MILITARY
DISTINCTION AND OF HONOR

But back to 1780 and the battlefield, where a bloody sun sank over a hill teeming with life and littered with the dead and dying. The loot, such as it was, passed into various hands. Cleveland, who had lost his big charger, Roebuck, in the battle, was given Ferguson's white stallion. Shelby got a second silver whistle, a larger ceremonial one, and Sevier took home Ferguson's silken sash. One of Lacey's men got the major's silver watch, reportedly as large as a turnip. And the sword with the inscription on the blade ended up in the hands of William Lenoir. It had a hilt of coin silver, and was, perhaps, the most valuable trophy of all. How Lenoir acquired it, he never made clear. Perhaps he was afraid someone would contest his right to it. Years later he did note, however, that because of the victory "many militia officers procured swords who could not possibly get any before."

Because of the lateness of the hour, the victors slept that night upon the battlefield. They were exhausted, and, despite the gnawing in their bellies and the groans of the wounded, they slept hard. The sword of the Lord and of Gideon had proved to be a mighty weapon, and they were well content.

But amid the noises of the night, one wounded man forced himself to finish a little chore. A Tory, he had been scrawling a record of each day's events in a small, brown, arithmetic book bound in calfskin. There wasn't much space for writing so each entry had been short.

The book was later found on the mountain. The final entry reads:

October ye 6th —

We marched off Toward Tryon old courthouse And camped near kings mountain; from thence we march to the high Pinacle of K [illegible] where we thought we would camp But Adverse fortune confused our

Imaginations, for the 7th of Octor. the cursed rebels came upon us, Killed and took us every Soul and so
My dear friends, I bid you farewell for I am started to the warm country.

The little book bears no name.

7

The Road to Yorktown

Sustaining the Patriots during their thirty-two hours of almost continuous marching before the battle was the thought that when they "got" Ferguson they would also get his supplies and thus enjoy a change from parched corn and toasted cow-bags. So intense was this vision of a banquet to come, that in 1830 an elderly veteran confused fancy with fact and actually described the meal that did not follow the victory. In a long ballad, he wrote:

> Apicius! what a feast there was,
>   blended of strong and sweet
> Cured venison hams, Falstaffian pies
>   and fat pigs' pickled feet

Unhappily, as has been noted, Ferguson's cupboard was almost as bare as the backwoodsmen's corn bags. There was little to eat on King's Mountain and the victors rose next morning with hunger gnawing at their bellies. It was a bright, brisk day and frost lay lightly on dead men, dead horses and dead and dying leaves of maple and oak. Adding to the turmoil of the stomach was uneasiness over the whereabouts of Tarleton. Everyone half expected "Bloody Ban" to appear momentarily at the head of his ruthless dragoons. Handicapped by lack of food and ammunition, burdened with some eight hundred prisoners, the rebel army was in no condition to take on Tarleton.

Nevertheless, there was much to be done before the army could head for the hills. It was decided to destroy the seventeen baggage wagons captured. To have taken them along would have slowed the march. So the wagons were pulled across the campfires and allowed to burn. The wounded would be carried in horse litters — a sort of hammock made of blankets and stretched between two horses. Much of the early morning was spent in constructing them. Fortunately, in the woods around the hill were plenty of small saplings from which litter poles could be fashioned. There were, of course, no plans to carry the enemy wounded. Most would have to die, but, contrary to much that has been written, they were not left untended on the battlefield. Captain dePeyster, in his official report to Lord Cornwallis, states clearly:

> Our wounded are left at one Wilsons, 4 miles this side of the place of action. They are without body cloths or blankets, and I fear the man who attends them [is] without medicine and is not sufficiently capable.

There is nothing to indicate that Lord Cornwallis troubled himself very much about these wounded men, nor is there any record of how many survived. Many, doubtless, were in the condition of one Tory examined on the mountain. A bullet had entered his forehead, passed through the head and out the back, yet the man still lived. He was sitting upright with his back to a large rock. When moved, however, he died instantly.

The wounded men were treated as gently as circumstances permitted. James Gray, for example, found an old friend among the Tories. He had been shot in the ankle and could barely hobble down to the branch for water. Gray administered such first aid as he could. Eventually, the man got home and was forever grateful.

Among the prisoners were some who had fought with Shelby at Musgrove Mill. Upon being questioned as to why they changed sides, they insisted they had no choice. It was either join Ferguson or see their homes destroyed. So convincing was their tale of impressment, Shelby ordered them released. Thereafter they were treated as friends if not as allies.

Also a prisoner was Virginia Paul, the surviving mistress. The mountain men had taken Ferguson's sword and sash, but no one was interested in his women. She remained with the army until it reached Quaker Meadows, and what happened to her after that is anyone's guess. One popular theory has it that somehow she rejoined Cornwallis's army, where she found a new protector.

One problem was what to do with the hundreds of muskets captured on the field. Estimates have ranged from 1,200 to 1,500. That careful reporter of specific detail, William Lenoir, had this to say on the subject:

> As we had no other way to bring the guns we had taken, the strong, healthy prisoners were directed to carry them, the officers and the weak and sickly being excused as well as the wounded. I stood by the pile of guns as they marched by to take them up, and I counted 725 men that carried guns, and many that carried two guns each.

Spurred by renewed rumors that Tarleton was fast approaching, the army finally marched about 10 A.M. Campbell remained behind with a burial detail. Two large pits were dug, one for the Patriots and one for the Tories, and the bodies were tumbled in without much ceremony. The work was hastily done for no one was in a mind to risk the living by tarrying too long with the dead.

James Collins, one of those assigned to the task, has left a description:

> They were thrown into convenient piles and covered with old logs, the bark of old trees, and rocks; yet not so as to secure them from becoming a prey to the beasts of the forest or the vultures of the air; and the wolves became so plenty that it was dangerous for any one to be out at night, for several miles around; also, the hogs in the neighborhood gathered in to the place to devour the flesh of men, so much that numbers chose to live on little meat rather than eat their hogs, though they were fat. Half the dogs in the country were said to be mad and were put to death. I saw, myself, in passing the place a few weeks after, all parts of the human frame lying scattered in every direction . . .

So disgraceful did the scene appear in time that in 1815, on the thirty-fifth anniversary of the battle, the residents of the region gathered on the mountain to rebury the bones of the dead. Since bones couldn't be classified as to character or politics, no segregation was possible. A monument, the first of several, was erected. One side did honor to the memory of Major Chronicle and the South Fork men who had died with him. Proof that time had begun its healing is evident in the fact that the other side of the shaft remembered Patrick Ferguson, a Scotsman who died far from home.

The men marched twelve miles that day and camped on a deserted plantation — the owner was a Tory — where they found a field planted in sweet potatoes. This, remarked one of the soldiers, "was most fortunate for not one in fifty of us had tasted food for the last two days and nights." But they had more than yellow potatoes to eat. The footmen, left behind at Green River, came up with a goodly supply of beef. According to Lenoir, "our men had suffered from fatigue and hunger for three days and were nearly famished."

Perhaps the big meal made everyone lazy and complacent, for next day the calvacade moved less than three miles. It was still a large body, at least two thousand strong. A number of men such as the South Fork soldiers and the South Carolinians broke off to go to their respective homes, but the addition of the foot-men and the prisoners more than compensated for the loss. Yet the lack of powder made it very vulnerable and safety seemed to increase with each step toward the blue mountains to the north and west.

Twenty miles were made on October 10th, and another twelve miles on the day following. They were in the neighborhood of Gilbert Town, and it was then that Captain dePeyster was permitted to write his report to Cornwallis. It concluded in this fashion:

> As this letter is to be read by the commanding officer, & I am not allowed to mention particulars, I have only to wish your Lordship may be pleased to think of us, particularly of the poor soldiers who have been suffering for some time past. I have the honor to be with due respect
>
> > My Lord
> > Your Lordships most
> > Obet Servt
> > A. DePeyster, Capt.

Colonel Campbell also did some writing that day, a general order to his men. It asked for a list by regiment of dead and wounded, and ordered that two hundred men plus officers be assigned to guard duty each day. And it concluded on this note:

"I must request the officers of all ranks in the army to endeavor to restrain the disorderly manner of slaughtering and disturbing the prisoners. If it cannot be prevented by moderate measures, such effectual punishment shall be executed upon delinquents as will put a stop to it."

Three days later he issued another order:

"It is with anxiety I hear the complaints of the inhabitants on account of the plundering parties who issue out of camp, and indiscriminately rob both Whig and Tory, leaving our friends, I believe, in a worse situation than the enemy would have done. I hope the officers will exert themselves in suppressing this abominable practice, degrading to the name of soldier, by keeping their soldiers close in camp and preventing their straggling off upon our marches."

Food was scarce. Lieutenant Allaire, still scribbling in his diary, waited until he was safely in Charleston before complaining about the lack of food for prisoners. Pumpkins became a staple — when sliced thin and fried they were considered "about the sweetest eating I ever had in my life."

If food was becoming harder to find, the fear of Tarleton was also decreasing. It seemed obvious that if "Bloody Ban" was on their tracks, he would have caught up with them. So, momentarily, that fear was put aside and upon reaching a plantation known as Bickerstaff's, northeast of Gilbert Town, the army decided it had time to administer justice.

Some of the junior officers presented a formal complaint to Campbell, alleging that among the prisoners were a number of murderers and house-burners. They asked that a court be convened to try the felons and that those found guilty be promptly executed before they could escape and commit more crimes.

According to Shelby, an "American officer paroled from Ninety-Six only the day before" arrived in camp and reported "he had seen eleven American citizens hung at that place within a few days past, merely for their attachment to the cause of their country."

The visitor's account "very much exasperated" the officers. The problem was how to give a facade of legality to their purpose which was, in part, revenge, and, in part, massive retaliation. The men believed, or at least said they did, that some hangings on their part would make the British less ready to use the noose. A visitor to camp produced a copy of a new law "authorizing two justices-of-the-peace to cause to be apprehended any citizen or Loyalist who might be found in arms against his country, and, if found guilty of treason, to order him to immediate execution without any pleading in the case."

Since the army was in Rutherford County and there were several county officials, including the sheriff, present, Campbell called a council of officers to try some of the prisoners. According to one witness, the jury was composed of "field officers and captains."

"They commenced trying them early in the morning," Shelby wrote, "beginning with the most atrocious offenders first who had committed murder deliberately in cold blood and destroyed the families of Whigs, burned down houses, and committed the most enormous crimes. They continued to try them until they had condemned 36 to be hung, and at two o'clock in the night following, commenced hanging them . . ."

Among those hung was Ambrose Mills. He, it will be remembered, was one of the few Tories actually identified as being present on the night Noah Hampton was murdered. Andrew Hampton, the avenging father, thus exacted his revenge despite any proof that Mills had anything to do with the act of murder per se. In the absence of such evidence, the charge was made that Mills had plotted to encourage the Cherokees to ravage the frontier.

Also among those convicted was James Crawford, the Watauga traitor who with young Sam Chambers had deserted at Carver's Gap and carried the news of the mountaineer army to Ferguson. Chambers wasn't charged because of his youth. Crawford was allowed to sweat a little and then was pardoned at the request of Sevier, who had served with him on the frontier against the Cherokees. After all, Sevier pointed out, it could be argued that whatever Crawford's intentions, his message had helped "tree the possum" on King's Mountain.

Lieutenant Allaire, an angry witness to the proceedings, said Mills and the others "died like Romans."

Only nine of those sentenced were executed. They were hung three at a time from the projecting limb of an oak tree. The scene was illuminated by pine torches and both prisoner and victor watched. Some of the more partisan rejoiced — one man wishing out loud that "every tree in the wilderness bore such fruit," but apparently most of the men quickly had enough. When the younger brother of a condemned man managed to cut his ropes while pretending to bid him farewell, not a shot was fired as the two prisoners ran into the dark forest.

Sensing the mood change, Shelby, Sevier and Cleveland decided to stop the executions. Campbell agreed when asked. The ropes were removed from the necks of the next three men, and orders were given to disperse. The party was over.

Whatever the justice of the summary executions, they seemed to have had a beneficial effect. Not only did the British stop hanging people out of hand, but the Tories lost any zeal for King George that might have remained to them. As far as the civil war in the Carolinas was concerned, except for a few die-hards, it ended at King's Mountain.

But the melodramatic events of the night weren't over by any means. One of those given a last-second pardon asked to talk to Shelby in private. His gratitude was such, he explained, that he felt it necessary to inform the Colonel that Tarleton would attack at dawn. A woman had come into camp earlier that evening with a message to the British officers to be alert when the attack was mounted. The word had been passed to some of the rank and file.

It seemed incredible, but given Tarleton's reputation as a hard rider, not impossible. Shelby quickly spread the alarm. As he told it later:

> The Americans immediately all mounted their horses and were ready to march as soon as it was light enough to see, for the night was exceptionally dark. As soon as they could see the way, they started directly for the mountains.

It was a tense and trying time, those first few hours. DePeyster added to the tension by riding up to Shelby and inquiring where they were going in such a hurry.

"To our natural element, the mountains," replied Shelby.

"You smell a rat," said dePeyster.

"We know all about it," said Shelby.

Shortly after daylight it began to rain — a driving, steady downpour that turned the little valley they were passing through into a roaring river. The water was waist deep at times, but the goal was to reach the upper Catawba and cross it before Tarleton could catch them. The march continued long after darkness fell. It was 10 P.M. before they reached the river. It was rising rapidly and there was no time to lose. Soon it would be impassable. The prisoners were forced into a column six men wide, and told to hold on to each other. Their lives depended upon themselves. According to Allaire, "all the men were worn out with fatigue and fasting — the prisoners having no bread or meat for two days before." Yet, he added, about one hundred prisoners escaped during the thirty-two-mile march that day.

Next morning the river had risen ten feet, and now offered an impassable barrier to Tarleton and everyone else. The mountaineers felt that Providence was still protecting them. This feeling of well-being was heightened when they camped at Quaker Meadows after fording the river. Major McDowell offered his rail fences for firewood, and they was immediately accepted. As Benjamin Sharp, a veteran of the campaign, remarked: "It was rather cold, being the last of October, and everyone from the Commander-in-Chief to the meanest private was as wet as if he had just been dragged through the Catawba river."

For once the British officers had nothing to complain about. They were invited to the McDowell home and treated as guests. The elderly mother of Charles and Joseph McDowell was hostess and a happy one. Earlier in the summer when her sons were fugitives beyond the mountains, some of these same officers had visited her and made threats as to what they would do to her sons when caught. Now, cold and miserable, they were back as prisoners — willing to accept hospitality from an old lady they had tried to torment.

The army rested next day, and reorganized. An urgent message from across the mountains made it necessary. The Cherokees, certain now that many of the frontiersmen were far away, were about to attack. Sevier and Shelby conferred. It was decided that Sevier would take most of their respective commands across the mountain as fast as possible. Shelby would go on with the prisoners and try to talk Gates — or whoever commanded the Continental army, if there was still such a thing — into taking action against the Indians similar to the expedition led by Rutherford in 1776.

Campbell sent many of his Virginians back with Sevier, but he remained with the army, which now largely consisted of Burke, Wilkes and Surrey County men under Cleveland, Winston and McDowell. In fact, there were almost as many prisoners as guards.

The army moved on, crossing over John's River and marching through Mulberry Gap to the lovely land near the head of the Yadkin since known as Happy Valley. Down the Yadkin they went, past old Fort Defiance where, in two years, Captain Lenoir would build a home that stands today, and on past the present city of Wilkesboro to the Moravian settlements where Winston-Salem now makes cigarettes.

And there they learned the whereabouts of Tarleton and Cornwallis. It was almost funny. While the mountaineers had been struggling through the rain, fording swollen rivers, and pushing themselves and their prisoners to the limits of endurance to get away from Tarleton, the entire British army had been enduring similar hardships to get away from the horde of barbarians that had so suddenly appeared from the mysterious lands of the western waters. As Reverend Doak would say, it had rained alike on the just and the unjust. While the Patriots went north as fast as possible, Cornwallis had fled south. The soil of North Carolina was free of invaders.

News of the victory at King's Mountain was spreading. General Gates, awaiting removal as commander in the south, sent a courier riding to Governor Jefferson of Virginia with dispatches. In his covering letter, Gates called the victory "great and glorious" and remarked hopefully: "We are now more than even with the enemy." Jefferson sent the tidings on to the Continental Congress.

The Congress was especially heartened to have good news at that particular juncture. For morale was at a low ebb indeed. The treason of Benedict Arnold had just been exposed and Major John André, the spy who had conspired with him, had just been hanged. On October 5, three days after the hanging and two days before the battle of King's Mountain, General Washington unburdened himself in a letter to General John Cadwalader:

> We have no Magazines, nor money to form them and in a little time we shall have no men [even] if we had money to pay them. We have lived on expedients until we can live no longer.

His mood changed with news of victory. In a general order Washington congratulated the army "on an important advantage lately obtained in North Carolina." It was, he added, "proof of the spirit and resources of the country."

Washington perhaps lacked the perspective to fully comprehend the importance of the battle won by citizens so far away. Exactly one year and twelve days later, at Yorktown, it would make more sense.

To those on the scene, however, the news had a more personal meaning. General Davidson put it very well in a letter to General Sumner:

"Ferguson, the great partisan, has miscarried."

2

Robert Henry and three of the South Fork boys were indirectly responsible for getting the news of Ferguson's defeat to Lord Cornwallis.

Henry's wounds were hurting him badly, so his friends decided to get him home as fast as possible. They rode across the battlefield and noticed that "in some places the dead lay thick and other places thin," and made five miles before halting for the night. Next morning, the day after the battle, they rode on to the South Fork. His friends "would not suffer me to ride the river," Henry reported, "but took me across in a canoe and hauled me home in a slide."

The pain was extreme but Henry's mother "made a poultice of wet ashes and applied it to my wounds. This gave me the first ease."

On Monday, the second day after the battle, some people came to visit the wounded hero. They called themselves "Neutralists," but in reality they were Tories. With considerable satisfaction, Henry listened as two friends, Hugh Erwin and Andrew Barry, gave their version of the battle. It went, says Henry, like this:

> *Tories:* Is it certain that Ferguson is killed and his army defeated and taken prisoner?
>
> *E and B:* It is certain for we saw Ferguson dead and his army prisoners.
>
> *Tories:* How many men had Ferguson?
>
> *E and B:* Nearly twelve hundred.
>
> *Tories:* Where did they get men enough to defeat him?
>
> *E and B:* They had the South Carolina and Georgia refugees, Colonel Graham's men, some from Virginia, some from the head of the Yadkin, some from the head of the Catawba, some from over the mountains, and some from everywhere else.

Tories: Tell us how it happened.

E and B: We met at Gilbert Town and found that foot soldiers couldn't overtake Ferguson, and we took between six and seven hundred horsemen, having as many or more footmen to follow, and we overtook Ferguson at King's Mountain, where we surrounded and defeated him.

Tories: Ah! That won't do. Between six and seven hundred to surround nearly twelve hundred. It would take more than two thousand to surround and take Ferguson.

E and B: But we were all of us blue hen's chickens.

Tories: There must have been of your horse and foot, in all, more than four thousand. We see what you're about — that is, to catch Lord Cornwallis napping.

The conversation ended. The "Neutralists" hurried away. It was only two hours after sunrise, but soon Henry heard that they crossed the flooded Catawba by swimming a horse along a canoe, and were heading for Charlotte as fast as they could ride.

The next installment was supplied by David Knox, a Patriot prisoner in Charlotte with the freedom of the village. He reported that on Monday afternoon, he was walking the street when he noticed an officer emerge from headquarters and stop to talk to the officer of the guard. The conversation went like this:

First Officer: Did you hear the news?

Officer of the Guard: No. What news?

First Officer: Ferguson is killed and his whole army defeated and taken prisoners.

Officer of the Guard: How can that be? Where did the men come from to do that?

> *First Officer:* Some of them were from South Carolina and Georgia, some from Virginia, some from the head of the Yadkin and the Catawba, and some from over the mountains. They met at Gilbert Town, about two thousand desperadoes on horseback calling themselves blue hen's chickens, and they overtook Ferguson at a place called King's Mountain, and there they killed Ferguson and defeated his army and took them prisoners.
>
> *Officer of the Guard:* Can this be true?
>
> *First Officer:* As true as the gospel, and we may look out for breakers.
>
> *Officer of the Guard:* God bless us!

Whereupon Knox, an ancestor of James Polk, a future President of the United States, jumped up on a pile of wood and crowed like a rooster.

"Day is at hand," he proclaimed for all who didn't know what a cock's crow meant.

Cornwallis would not, of course, have accepted the first reports of such a disaster without some confirmation. Isaac Shelby learned how it was received.

Some weeks after the battle, Shelby was at General Morgan's camp at a place called New Providence, when "a respectable, plain-looking old gentleman" told of being picked up by Cornwallis's men and questioned by Cornwallis himself. The "old man" had two sons fighting for the Rebels, so he was considered a good source of information.

"Who defeated Ferguson?" asked Cornwallis.

"The men from the west under Campbell, Shelby, Sevier and Cleveland," replied the Patriot, willingly enough.

"What is their number and where are they going?"

"My Lord," said the old man, "I understand they are three thousand strong and they are bearing down upon you."

This was confirmation enough. "The old man," said Shelby, "observed that his Lordship stepped a little to one side with Lord Rawdon, that in a few minutes the drums began to beat to arms throughout the camp, and a retreat was shortly commenced which continued all night in the utmost confusion, and as fast as waggons stalled or broke down they were ordered to be set on fire."

Tarleton has left an account of those bewildering days which, if not entirely objective, gives one British point of view:

> On the 10th, Earl Cornwallis gave orders to Lieutenant-Colonel Tarleton, to march with the light infantry, the British Legion, and a three pounder, to assist Major Ferguson, no certain intelligence having arrived at his defeat. Tarleton's instructions directed him to reinforce Ferguson wherever he could find him, and to draw his corps to the Catawba, if after the junction, advantage could not be obtained over the mountaineers; or, upon the certainty of his defeat, at all events to oppose the entrance of the victorious Americans into South Carolina. Accordingly, Tarleton marched to Smith's Ford, below the forks of the Catawba, where he received certain information of the melancholy fate of Major Ferguson.
>
> The destruction of Ferguson and his corps marked the period and the extent of the first expedition into North Carolina. . . . The King's troops left Charlotte town on the evening of the 14th, to march to the Catawba ford. Owing to the badness of the road, the ignorance of the guides, the darkness of the night, or from other unknown causes, the British rear guard destroyed or left behind near twenty waggons loaded with supplies from the army, a printing press, and other stores belonging to public departments, and the knapsacks of the light infantry and legion. Lieutenant colonel Tarleton had directed his troops to leave their

baggage with the army when sent upon the late expedition. The order for the move being unexpected at Charlotte town, the property of the absent was committed to the worst waggons, and was unfortunately lost. As soon as the British legion and the light infantry arrived at the Catawba ford, they were ordered to cross the river which they accomplished with some difficulty on account of a great fall rain. The royal forces remained two days in an anxious and miserable situation in the Catawba settlement, owing to a dangerous fever which suddenly attacked Earl Cornwallis, and to the want of forage and provisions. When the physicians declared his lordship's health would endure the motion of a waggon, Colonel Lord Rawdon, the second in command, directed the King's troops to cross Sugar Creek where some supplies might be obtained from the country.

The retreat stopped at Winnsboro, South Carolina, on October 29, having covered some seventy miles during the two-week nightmare. Ironically, a courier found the retreating army with a message from Major General Alexander Leslie at Portsmouth, Virginia. Leslie had the pleasure and honor of informing his Lordship that with 2,500 men he had landed in the Chesapeake Bay area in obedience to his Lordship's desires. What did his Lordship want him to do now?

Sir Henry Clinton had dispatched Leslie from New York, three days after King's Mountain, with instructions to "pursue such measures as you shall judge most likely to answer the purpose of this expedition, the principal object of which is to make a diversion in favour of Lieutenant-general Earl Cornwallis, who, by the time you arrive there, will probably be acting in the back parts of North Carolina."

His Lordship was too ill to reply. Lord Rawdon, acting for Cornwallis and on his instructions, wrote a long letter to Leslie which was at once an apology and an explanation. He reviewed Cornwallis's hopes and plans for the campaign, and then detailed the disaster that had befallen them:

Major Ferguson, with about eight hundred militia collected from the neighborhood of Ninety-Six, had previously marched into Tryon county to protect our friends, who were supposed to be numerous there, and it was intended that he should cross the Catawba river and endeavor to preserve tranquillity in the rear of the army. A numberous army now appeared on the frontiers, drawn from Nolachucki and other settlements beyond the mountains, whose very names had been unknown to us. A body of these, joined by the inhabitants of the ceded lands in Georgia, made a sudden and violent attack upon Augusta. The post was gallantly defended by Lieutenant Colonel Brown until he was relieved by the activity of Lieutenant Colonel Cruger; but Major Ferguson, by endeavoring to intercept the enemy in their retreat, unfortunately gave time for fresh bodies of men to pass the mountains and to unite in a corps far superior to that which he commanded. They came up with him, and after a sharp action, entirely defeated him. Ferguson was killed and all his party either taken or slain.

By the enemy's having secured all the passes on the Catawba, Lord Cornwallis — who was waiting at Charlotteburg for a convoy of stores — received but confused accounts of the affair for some time, but at length the truth reached him, and the delay equally with the precautions the enemy had taken to keep their victory from his knowledge, gave Lord Cornwallis great reason to fear for the safety of Ninety-Six. To secure that district was indispensable for the security of the rest of the province, and Lord Cornwallis saw no means of effecting it but by passing the Catawba river with his army for it was so weakened by sickness that it could not bear detachment.

Rawdon indicated that Cornwallis would like to order Leslie to re-embark his men and sail to Charleston, but hesitated to do so for fear it might interfere with plans Clinton, the official commander in chief, might have. He suggested Leslie do as he thought best. Shortly thereafter, however, Cornwallis recovered his courage and ordered Leslie to sail south. He reached Charleston on December 16, and then marched north to Camden with most of his men.

The grand plan was in shambles. Instead of a diversion, Leslie had become a replacement. In a letter to Clinton dated October 29, Rawdon, on behalf of Cornwallis, told his superior:

> The defeat of Major Ferguson had so dispirited this part of the country . . . that Lieutenant Colonel Cruger sent information to Earl Cornwallis that the whole district had determined to submit as soon as the rebels should enter it. From these circumstances, from the consideration that delay does not extinguish our hopes in North Carolina, and from the long fatigue of the troops, which made it seriously requisite to give some refreshment to the army, Earl Cornwallis has resolved to remain for the present in a position which may secure the frontiers without separating his forces.

There was, however, amid the gloom at least one bright spot: the chiefs of 2,500 Cherokees had promised to march immediately against the settlers of "the Watoga, Holstein, Caintuck, Nolachuckie, Cumberland and Green Rivers."

Cornwallis had learned to respect the Backwater Men even if he had not yet learned how to spell the names of their rivers.

3

John Sevier recrossed the mountains even more rapidly than on his outward march. There was no need for caution going home, and much need for speed. He paused long enough to kiss his bride and ascertain that she was pregnant before pushing on to meet with Arthur Campbell of Washington County, Virginia, to plan an offensive war. A rendezvous was arranged on the French Broad River west of present-day Asheville.

Because he had his King's Mountain men already under arms, Sevier was first in the field with three hundred men. He arrived at the French Broad early in December, a heroic march considering the weather and the high country. Hearing nothing from Campbell, his senior, Sevier sent out his scouts. Soon they reported that a Cherokee war party enroute to the settlements was just on the other side of the river.

A man of instant decision, Sevier crossed the French Broad and made a forced march toward the Indian camp on Boyd's Creek. At sunrise on December 16, the scouts reported the Cherokees had just moved out. Sevier ordered the scouts to chase the Cherokees, pretend to attack, and then retreat in panic as soon as a counterattack was launched.

The feint had worked well at Musgrove's Mill — why not against the Indians who had fallen for it way back in '76 at the battle of Island Flats?

While waiting, Sevier spread his men in a long line, the left wing under Major Jesse Walton and the right under Major Jonathan Tipton. Sevier commanded the center. When the advancing Indians hit it, the two wings were supposed to close in and around, trapping the whole party.

All went well at first. The Cherokees chased the retreating scouts and ran blindly into the trap. They suspected nothing until Sevier's men rose to their feet and fired. Walton's wing closed in quickly, but Tipton wasn't fast enough. The Indians spotted the hole and fled through it into a trackless swamp where it was every man for himself. Complete victory was thus denied, but the Watauga men took thirteen scalps, a number of rifles, and all the plunder they had accumulated. In the loot were several proclamations issued by Sir Henry Clinton and other British officers — proof positive, so the men decided, that the Indian uprising was part of the British master plan of conquest.

One month and nine days had passed since King's Mountain. Not a man of Sevier's force was as much as wounded. It was a victory for legend builders, and in years to come they made use of it. The Indians were increased to a thousand, and Sevier's force cut in half to make his achievement even greater.

It was enough to annoy a jealous Arthur Campbell without being exaggerated. In his official report of the campaign he devoted one sentence to the battle of Boyd's Creek. And then he noted:

"After this action, the Wattago corps thought proper to retreat to an island in the river. On the 22d I crossed the French River, and found the Wattago men in great want of provisions. We gave them a supply from our small stock, and the next day made a forced march toward the Tenasse . . ."

It would seem that Campbell's spelling of proper names was as creative as most of Cornwallis's.

The expedition continued deep into what is now central Tennessee. The towns of Chote, Sictogo, Tuskeego, Chilhowee, Toque, Micliqua, Kaiatee, Saltoga, Telico, Hiwassee, and Chistowee — containing "upwards of one thousand houses" — were destroyed. "Not less than fifty thousand bushels of corn and large quantities of other kinds of provisions" were destroyed — after, of course, deducting such amounts needed by an army living off the country.

Arthur Campbell wrote in his official report:

"Never did a people so happily situated act more foolishly, in losing their livings and their country at a time when an advantageous neutrality was held out to them, but such are the consequences of British seduction. The enemy in my absence did some mischief in Powell's Valley, and on the Kentucky path near Cumberland Gap, besides three children that they scalped on Halstein, one of the perpetrators of which we killed on our return, and retook a number of horses."

4

Isaac Shelby left the remains of the mountaineer's army, and the remains of its corps of prisoners, at the Moravian settlements founded by Bishop Spangenberg, and rode out in search of Daniel Morgan. He found him at a place called New Providence on the border of South Carolina near Charlotte.

Morgan was born about 1736 somewhere along the eastern seaboard. His parents were from Wales, the father an ironmaster. Little is known about his early life, but by 1753 young Daniel was on his own, working his way south through Pennsylvania. He was a big man, six feet two, and strong. By the time he reached Virginia he was a wagoner, a rough, tough profession. He needed all his toughness in 1755 when he signed on with General Edward Braddock to fight the French and Indians. In the disaster, Morgan helped evacuate the wounded and was present when the dying Braddock promised:

"We shall know better how to deal with them another time."

The British didn't profit much by the lesson, but Morgan did. Because of his leadership qualities and his fighting zeal, he won a commission in the British army. Shortly afterwards he was ambushed by Indians. A bullet hit him in the neck and emerged through his left cheek, taking several teeth along with it. Yet Morgan wheeled his horse and rode to safety. Scarred for life, and beset by crippling attacks of sciatica, he nevertheless lost none of his zest for living. As a brawler he was undisputed champion of a wide area until he met Miss Abigail Curry. She married him, gentled him considerably, and taught him a lot about reading, writing and arithmetic.

With the coming of the Revolution, Morgan was back in the

saddle. He led a party of frontiersmen to help raise the siege of Boston. Their hunting shirts and long rifles made them famous. Later he took part in the unsuccessful invasion of Canada. At the head of his riflemen, he fought his way into walled Quebec during the final, desperate battle. Cut off, he had to surrender, but was paroled in time to play a decisive role in the Battle of Saratoga that made Gates a hero. When Congress failed to give him the promotion he thought he deserved, Morgan resigned his commission and went home. He was no politician and had no desire to be one. Following Charleston, he had second thoughts about duty, and returned to the army. Belatedly, Congress made him a brigadier general. But the war marked time as far as the Continental army was concerned until Nathaniel Greene arrived to replace Gates.

Shelby thought Morgan a man of his own mold, the kind of commander his independent mountaineers would follow cheerfully to hell and back. If Morgan could be given authority to attack Ninety-Six and Augusta, the British line of communications with the Cherokees would be cut. Without trade goods and ammunition, the Indians would soon resign their hostile ways, Shelby believed.

The idea of an independent command appealed very much to Morgan when Shelby presented his plan. That he would be reinforced by some of the men who won King's Mountain was another inducement. All he needed, he said, was permission from Gates or Greene.

Gates was due on a visit. Shelby waited a few days for him to arrive. The two men sat on a log and Shelby talked. Gates was agreeable, subject, he said, to the approval of the Board of War for North Carolina which, officially, controlled the militia of the state. Again approval was obtained, and Shelby went home satisfied.

Within hours of his departure, General Greene arrived to take command of the Southern Department. Greene was tactful. He dismissed an effort to hold a board of inquiry into Gates' conduct at Camden, and let him retire in honor to his Virginia farm. Greene also confirmed the plans devised by Shelby for Morgan. The new general was given command of various units including a regiment of light dragoons, and ordered "to proceed to the west side of the Catawba River." All militia in the area were under his control. The total force was to be employed against the enemy "either offensively or defensively as your own prudence and discretion may direct."

It was exactly what Shelby wanted, what Morgan wanted. But it puzzled the hell out of Cornwallis. The idea of dividing one's force in the face of a superior enemy was, to him, astonishing.

Eventually, however, after Leslie's troops had come up from Charleston and Tarleton had recovered from his bout with the fever, Cornwallis began to move. Reinforcements were sent to Camden. Cornwallis moved north toward King's Mountain from his base at Winnsboro. And Tarleton was reinforced and told to get going after Morgan.

"Push him to the utmost," said Cornwallis. "No time is to be lost."

Tarleton was eager. He replied: "I must either destroy Morgan's corps or push it before me over Broad River toward King's Mountain."

They were trying to trap the "Old Wagoner," as Morgan was popularly known.

It seemed to work. After several days of marching in heavy rains that caused the Broad to flood, Morgan found himself backed into a corner near Hannah's Cowpens — the spot where the mountaineers had paused briefly on their way to meet Ferguson. He assumed, and so did Tarleton, that Cornwallis was waiting close by on the other side. It was a grim prospect to fight with one's back to a swollen river but to have an ever larger enemy force waiting on the other side made it a simple decision.

Morgan rode out to survey the ground. It lay upward as Tarleton would approach, a grassy slope rising gently for four hundred yards, leveling off for a few feet, and rising again for six .

hundred yards to a crest. On the other side it sloped off sharply to the Broad River some five miles away.

"On this ground," said Morgan, "I will defeat the British or lay my bones."

His officers were astonished. They pointed out that the flanks would be open to Tarleton's dragoons, and the entire force could be encircled by an army superior in numbers. But Morgan was unshaken — he knew *his* men and he had a pretty good idea of Tarleton's hell-for-leather personality.

Even more shocking to the Continental officers present was Morgan's planned use of his militia. All knew that militia was worthless, but Morgan intended to put them in his front lines.

The night before the battle, Morgan rested his men, and fed them well. Then he walked among them, talking as one frontiersman to another. He explained his battle plan in detail, and made fun of "Banny." He even pulled up his shirt to show his scars from the lashing he had received under Braddock. Then he told everyone to turn in early and get a good rest. He would see they were awakened in time to eat a hearty breakfast before the battle.

All that night the militia units straggled in to give Morgan the help promised by Shelby. When the sun went up on the morning of January 17, 1781, he had collected an estimated one thousand men. As many as two hundred of them may have been veterans of King's Mountain, according to Professor Bobby G. Moss of Limestone College, but there is no way to be sure. Tarleton, driving forward without rest, had approximately eleven hundred men, none of them Tory militia. In regulars he had a three to one advantage over Morgan, and he was supremely confident.

Tarleton's troops were awakened at 3 A.M. and set to marching. About dawn, his advance patrols made contact with an American patrol, and each raced back to tell the news. Tarleton was jubilant with his information — Morgan, waiting in force, on an exposed hill with his flanks unprotected? It seemed too good to be true.

When his scouts came in, Morgan loosed a shout:

"Boys, get up. Banny is coming."

There was still time to eat the breakfast Morgan had promised. It had been cooked the night before. The troops were pleased. Morgan was their kind of man. In good humor, they took their positions.

The old campaigner had devised a unique battle plan involving three lines. The first consisted of 150 picked sharpshooters under Majors Joseph McDowell and John Cunningham of Georgia. Its job was to fire two shots at the advancing British, then retreat to *and through* the second line, which was composed of the rest of the militia under Colonel Andrew Pickens. Those men were told to wait until the Redcoats came near and then to fire two shots also. Having fired them, Pickens was to lead the second line laterally to its left and out of sight behind the hill. They were supposed to circle the hill to the rear and reappear on the American right. Meanwhile, the third line, posted near the crest of the hill and composed of Continental army units that had survived Camden, was to stand its ground. In reserve, out of sight behind the hill, Morgan had about 125 mounted men under the command of Colonel William Washington.

The first of several assumptions on which the battle plan depended was that Tarleton would charge headlong upon seeing the enemy. In fact, he first sent in fifty dragoons with their famous sabers bared. Amid war whoops from the backwoodsmen, the sharpshooters in the grass emptied fifteen saddles. The dragoons turned back. But Tarleton saw the hidden shooters get up and rush back to the second line, and he saw them keep going *through* the second line. That was enough. He ordered the entire British line forward on the double.

After that the battle went more or less as planned. Pickens's men fired twice and retreated to the left. Encouraged, Tarleton kept coming up the long hill. Some of the militia seemed to move faster than anticipated. Lieutenant Joseph Hughes, of King's Mountain fame, rushed ahead of them and turned them back. Everyone then marched sedately to the right side arriving on the flank at just the critical moment. For Tarleton had momentarily broken the Continentals. Desperate efforts by their commander, Colonel John Howard, and Morgan, stopped them, however, and they wheeled and fired a deadly volley into the oncoming British. In the same instant on the right, the militia opened up with a flanking fire, and Colonel Washington brought his cavalry around and came charging in from the rear. In an instant apparent British victory turned into complete defeat, and the Americans were shouting their grim reminder: "Tarleton's quarter."

The cocky colonel had a narrow personal escape and was chased from the field with less than two hundred dragoons to his name. Left behind were one hundred and ten dead, two hundred wounded, and some six hundred prisoners. Morgan lost twelve dead, sixty-one wounded. When Cornwallis heard about it, he penned a note to Lord Rawdon which began:

"The late affair has almost broke my heart."

More than his heart was broken. For Cornwallis was now on the road to Yorktown. Forgetting his master plan, he burned his wagons and chased Greene across North Carolina like a madman. When Greene wouldn't fight, Morgan resigned and went home. A general of George Washington's type, Greene won no battles but he kept his army in the field. When at last Cornwallis brought him to a showdown at Guilford Courthouse near modern Greensboro, Greene soon withdrew from the field but Cornwallis was too exhausted to continue. He retreated to Wilmington, and then went north to seek safety with Benedict Arnold, who had landed a British army in Virginia. Greene went the other way, to South Carolina and ultimately to Charleston. A poet described the action in this verse:

Cornwallis led a country dance,
The like was never seen, sir,
Much retrograde and much advance
And all with General Greene, sir

It was as if both sides had their fill of North Carolina, where men fought when and where and how they pleased. And won.

Epilogue

Whitetop Mountain

In the twenty-third year of the independence of the United States, and of the eighteenth century the ninety-ninth, there gathered on Whitetop Mountain several men who had fought at King's Mountain.

Major — now Brigadier General — Joseph McDowell was there. So was Captain David Vance, now clerk of court of Buncombe County. The two men had been appointed by the State of North Carolina to survey and mark its boundary line with the new State of Tennessee.

Chief surveyor for the project was Robert Henry. As a youth of sixteen he had been wounded by a bayonet at King's Mountain. He was now a surveyor and attorney of note in Buncombe County.

On hand also was Gideon Lewis as chief guide. He knew the mountains like no other, and had served as a courier in those desperate weeks before the gathering on the Watauga at Sycamore Shoals.

Much had happened since McDowell, Sevier, Shelby and

Campbell had led their men across the mountains to combine with Cleveland and Lenoir.

Item. Campbell had performed bravely at Guilford Courthouse and was fighting under la Fayette in Virginia when in August of 1781 he died of natural causes.

Item. Cleveland had been captured by the Tories in 1781 and was about to be hanged when rescued. He had since moved to Tugalo in western South Carolina, an area he first explored when returning from his horse-hunting expedition to the Cherokees years before. He was now a judge, but folks said he tended to fall asleep on the bench.

Item. Lenoir now lived at Fort Defiance in Happy Valley on the upper Yadkin after narrowly failing election as governor of North Carolina. His daughter, Patsy, would marry Israel Pickens, a future governor of Alabama. Lenoir's friend, Jesse Franklin, who had fought with him at King's Mountain, would become governor of North Carolina in 1820.

Item. Sevier had served as governor of the lost State of Franklin and was now governor of Tennessee. He would serve six terms in that capacity.

Item. Shelby had removed to Kentucky and in 1792 had become that state's first governor. He would serve again in 1812 and lead an army of riflemen to defeat the British and Indians at the battle of the Thames River in Canada.

McDowell had become a Congressman as well as a general, but in 1799 his task was to get the surveying crew to work. They had met at a point where the boundaries of North Carolina and Tennessee intersect the Virginia line. From that spot on Whitetop, a spur of Stone Mountain, the crew would go westward along the crest until it reached the boundary of the Indian Territory in the Great Smokies.

From the moment the men assembled, the chainmen, axemen, markers, and pack-horsemen began asking questions about the King's Mountain expedition, now nineteen years old. Soon they requested that either Vance or McDowell give them "a connected narrative." Vance agreed to do so after comparing notes with McDowell, Henry and Lewis. On the first "wet day," he promised, the story would be told.

The wet day wasn't long in coming. Snug in their bark shelter, the men settled down to hear the truth about a campaign that had become legendary in their lifetime. Also present was Mussentine Matthews, a third commissioner, who had a reputation for cynicism and perhaps an inferiority complex where Vance and McDowell were concerned.

Vance, whose grandson, Zebulon, would be the Civil War governor of North Carolina, began by outlining conditions in 1780. While mistaken on some points where he had no personal knowledge, his account was basically correct. So was his description of the battle. He concluded his tale on that rainy day atop the Blue Ridge with this bit of braggadocio:

> We had not a coward to face the hill that day; they all faded off until, within ten minutes of the battle, the last coward left us. Our equals were scarce and our superiors hard to find. This is the most particular and accurate account, my friends, that I can give you.

For reasons not explained, Matthews took issue with the story told by Vance. He is quoted as having said:

> Ah! you would have been a formidable and destructive set of blue hen's chickens if each of you had been provided with a good stick. When anybody pretends to tell the story of that transaction, it would be to his credit to play the game of shut mouth.

McDowell, a hero of Cowpens as well as King's Mountain, replied at length to Matthews. He sketched the conditions existing following the fall of Charleston and the defeat of Gates at Camden, and speculated as to what would have happened had Ferguson won the day at King's Mountain. And he did a little boasting in the style Davy Crockett would soon make famous:

We *were* the bravest of the brave. We *were* a formidable flock of blue hen's chickens of the game blood, of indomitable courage, strangers to fear. We *were* well provided with sticks; we made the egg shells — British and Tory skulls — fly like onion peelings in a windy day. The blue cocks flapped their wings and crowed.

Continuing, McDowell compared the battle to Thermopylae and found no parallel. Leonidas and his army were defeated, he pointed out. After again reviewing what defeat at King's Mountain would have meant to the cause of freedom, he summed up:

In short, Ferguson's defeat was the turning point in American affairs. The loss of this battle would, in all probability, have been the loss of American Independence and the liberty we now enjoy. I never on any occasion feel such dignified pride as when I think that my name counts as one of the number that faced the hill at King's Mountain that day of battle.

The only sound when he stopped talking was the steady beat of the rain.

Acknowledgments

The preparation of this book may have been a labor of love, but it was also hard work. Several individuals lightened the load along the way and them I would like to thank.

Miss Margaret Harper of Lenoir pointed me in the right direction; Mrs. Mildred McDowell Jones of Happy Valley helped me sort out the McDowells; Eugene Allen Poe of Lenoir and Ms. Faunie Lenoir of Happy Valley set me straight on Lenoir family history; and Fred Cranford of Morganton told me how to find Quaker Meadows.

Miss Peggy Smith in the North Carolina Room of the University of North Carolina Library at Chapel Hill was of great assistance. Very helpful was James J. Anderson, the able historian at King's Mountain National Military Park. Robert W. Allison of the Joseph Regenstein Library at the University of Chicago provided timely data on Isaac Shelby.

Deserving special mention are my handsome son, Jon, and my ever-loving wife, Faye. Jon accompanied me from Sycamore Shoals in eastern Tennessee to the little ridge called King's Mountain in northern South Carolina. As a "pilot" he was excellent even if he insisted on climbing Roan Mountain *twice*. Faye did the maps and the listening.

Finally, thanks go to my editor, Llewellyn Howland III, who, with faith and tact, helped me through some very rough country of another kind.

Bibliography

Abernathy, Thomas Perkins. *From Frontier to Plantation in Tennesee*. Chapel Hill, N.C.: 1932.

Agniel, Lucian. *The Late Affair Has Almost Broke My Heart*. Riverside, Conn.: 1972.

Alden, John. *The South in the Revolution*. Baton Rouge, La.: 1957.

Annals of America, Vol. 2. Chicago: 1968.

Bailey, J. D. *Commanders at King's Mountain*. Gaffney, S.C.: 1932.

Bakeless, John. *Daniel Boone*. Harrisburg, Pa.: 1963.

Bass, Robert D. *The Green Dragoon*. New York: 1957.

Boatner, Mark M. *Encyclopedia of the American Revolution*. New York: 1966.

Brown, Frank C. *Folklore of North Carolina*. Durham, N.C.: 1962.

Brown, John P. *Old Frontiers*. Kingsport, Tenn.: 1938.

Caruthers, E. W. *Some Account of the Regulation*. Greensboro, N.C.: 1842.

Chidsey, Donald Barr. *The Loyalists*. New York: 1973.

———. *The War in the South*. New York: 1969.

Clark, Walter. *State Records of North Carolina*. Charlotte, N.C.: 1905.

Collins, James. *Autobiography of a Revolutionary War Soldier*. Clinton, La.: 1859.

Commager, Henry Steele, and Morris, Richard B. *The Spirit of Seventy-Six*. New York and Indianapolis: 1958.

Crane, Verner W. *The Southern Frontier, 1670–1732.* Durham, N.C.: 1928.

Davidson, Donald. *The Tennessee.* New York: 1946.

DeMond, Robert O. *The Loyalists of North Carolina during the Revolution.* Durham, N.C.: 1940.

DePeyster, John Watts. *The Affair at King's Mountain.* New York: 1880.

Dictionary of American Biography, 21 Vols. New York: 1943.

Dictionary of National Biography, 63 Vols. London: 1885–1901.

Draper, Lyman C. *King's Mountain and Its Heroes.* Baltimore: 1967.

Echenrode, H. J. *The Revolution in Virginia.* Hamden, Conn.: 1964.

Falmsbee, Stanley J., Corlew, Robert E., and Mitchell, Enoch L. *Tennessee: A Short History.* Knoxville, Tenn.: 1969.

Ferguson, James. *Two Scottish Soldiers.* Aberdeen: 1888.

Freeman, Douglas Southall. *George Washington.* New York: 1948.

Fries, Adelaide L. *Records of the Moravians in North Carolina,* Vol. 1. Raleigh, N.C.: 1968.

Henderson, Felix. *Echoes of Happy Valley,* Durham, N.C.: 1962.

Henry, Robert, and Vance, David. *Narrative of the Battle of Cowan's Ford and Narrative of the Battle of King's Mountain.* Greensboro, N.C.: 1891.

Irving, Washington. *Life of Washington,* 5 Vols. New York: 1855–59.

Kimball, Marie. *Jefferson: War and Peace.* New York: 1947.

Kincaid, Robert L. *The Wilderness Road.* New York: 1947.

Lefler, Hugh T., and Powell, William S. *Colonial North Carolina.* New York: 1973.

————, and Newsome, Albert Ray. *North Carolina.* Chapel Hill, N.C.: 1954.

Lenoir, William. *Family Papers Collection.* University of North Carolina Library, Chapel Hill.

MacKenzie, George C. *King's Mountain.* National Park Service Historical Handbook Series No. 22, 1955.

Mahon, John K. *The War of 1812.* Gainesville, Fla.: 1972.

Meyer, Duane. *The Highland Scots of North Carolina.* Chapel Hill, N.C.: 1957.

Mooney, James. *Myths of the Cherokees.* Washington, D.C.: 1900.

Moore, Frank. *Diary of the Revolution.* New York: 1858.

———. *Songs & Ballads of the American Revolution.* New York: 1856.

O'Meara, Walter. *Guns at the Fork.* Englewood, N.J.: 1965.

Percy, Albert. *Virginia's Unsung Victory in the Revolution.* Madison Road, Va.: 1965.

Ramsey, J. G. M. *Annals of Tennessee.* Charleston, S.C.: 1853.

Rankin, John. *The American Revolution.* New York: 1964.

Ray, Worth S. *Tennessee Cousins.* Baltimore: 1968.

Roosevelt, Theodore. *The Winning of the West* (Abridged Edition). New York: 1963.

Ross, Malcolm. *The Cape Fear.* New York: 1965.

Rouse, Parke, Jr. *The Great Wagon Road.* New York: 1973.

Savage, Henry, Jr. *River of the Carolinas: The Santee.* Chapel Hill, N.C.: 1968.

Schenck, David. *North Carolina, 1780–81.* Raleigh, N.C.: 1889.

Shelby, Isaac. *Autobiography.* (Unpublished manuscript, Durrett Collection, The Joseph Regenstein Library, University of Chicago.)

Sosin, Jack M. *The Revolutionary Frontier.* New York: 1967.

Starr, Emmet. *History of the Cherokee Indians and Their Legends and Folklore.* Oklahoma City: 1921.

Tarleton, Banastre. *A History of the Campaign of 1780 and 1781 in the Southern Provinces of North Carolina.* London: 1787.

Thompson, Ernest Trice. *Presbyterians in the South*, Vol. I. Richmond, Va.: 1963.

Treacy, M. F. *Prelude to Yorktown.* Chapel Hill, N.C.: 1963.

Turner, Frederic Jackson. *The Frontier in American History.* New York: 1920.

Van Doren, Carl. *Secret History of the Revolution.* New York: 1941

Van Every, Dale. *A Company of Heroes.* New York: 1962.

———. *Forth to the Wilderness.* New York: 1963.

Ward, Christopher. *The War of the Revolution.* New York: 1952.

Wheeler, John Hill. *Historical Sketches of North Carolina.* Baltimore: 1964.

Wheeler, Richard. *Voices of 1776.* New York: 1972.

White, Katherine Keough. *The King's Mountain Men.* Baltimore: 1966.

Willcox, William B. *Portrait of a General, Sir Henry Clinton in the War of Independence*. New York: 1964.

Woodmason, Charles. *The Carolina Backcountry on the Eve of the Revolution*. Chapel Hill, N.C.: 1953.